Ancient Egyptian Religion

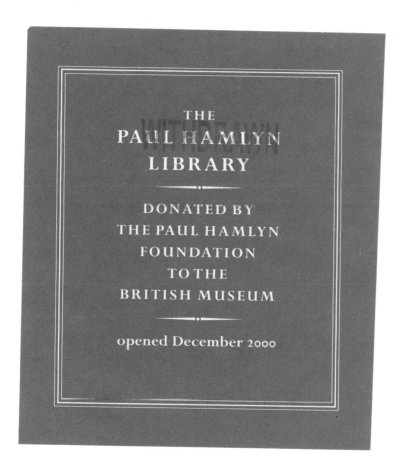

Ancient Egyptian Religion

Stephen Quirke

Dover Publications, Inc., New York

To the memory of Eileen

© 1992 Trustees of the British Museum
Published by British Museum Press
A division of The British Museum Company Ltd
46 Bloomsbury Street, London, WC1B 3QQ

Reprinted 1995, 1997

BRITISH LIBRARY CATALOGUING-IN-PUBLICATION DATA
A catalogue record for this book is available from
the British Library

Designed by Tim Higgins

Set in Compugraphic Galliard and Sabon by BP Integraphics Ltd.,
Bath, and Printed in Great Britain by The Bath Press, Bath

Acknowledgements

This book owes much to the constant cooperation of my colleagues in the Department of
Egyptian Antiquities at the British Museum, in particular to Carol Andrews, and to the
inspirational works of, above all, Alexandre Piankoff, Oleg Berlev, Jan Assmann, James
Allen and Erik Hornung. I am especially grateful in the production of this book to
Christine Barratt for the map and line drawings, to Peter Hayman for the photography
and to Rachel Rogers for the editing of the volume at every stage. All opinions and errors
remain of course my own responsibility.

FRONT COVER View through the central colonnade in the Hypostyle Hall at Karnak,
conceived in the reign of Amenhotep III and constructed under Sety I and Ramses II.
Photo: Graham Harrison.
BACK COVER Osiris figure with hollow interior to contain the *Book of the Dead* of
Hunefer. 19th Dynasty, *c.* 1275 BC; painted wood, of unknown provenance. H. 82 cm.
EA 9861.

Contents

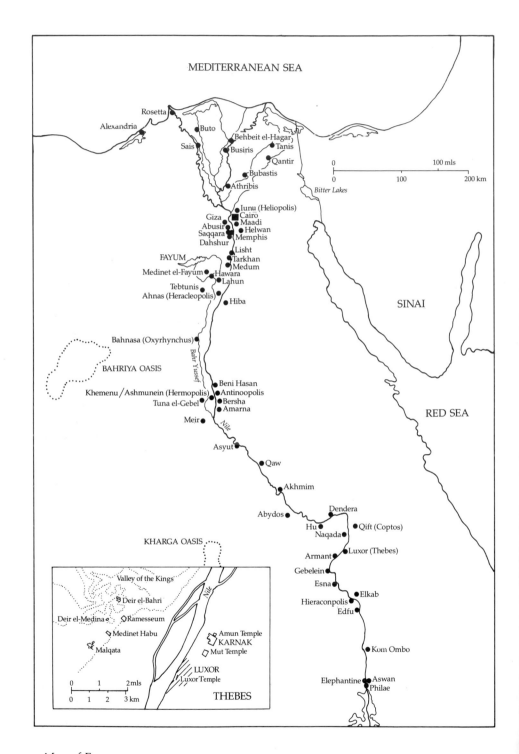

1 Map of Egypt.
Drawn by Christine Barratt.

INTRODUCTION

Knowing Egyptian Beliefs

INDIVIDUALS OR COMMUNITIES, WHEN FACED with lifestyles different from their own, tend either to accept them as a part of their own being or reject them as alien and irreconcilable. The same applies to the study of past ways of life, though with the huge added problem that it is impossible to confront directly the relevant individuals in order to ask them why they behaved so differently from us. Thus we can either regard these people and their societies as different historical expressions of a common humanity, or we can exclude them as curiosities in which we have no share other than as external observers. In tending to the former view, this book performs a precarious balancing act, presenting a view of the past that can be accepted by modern readers as being part of ourselves while at the same time preserving a sense of astonishment at the ways in which it undoubtedly differs. The world of Egyptian gods and goddesses has suffered greatly from this conflict of attitudes. On the one hand it is usually considered alien, and in particular the animal, bird and hybrid forms of Egyptian deities have evinced disgust in the non-Egyptian world since at least the time of ancient Roman writers. On the other hand, it has often been presented by scholars who appear incapable, in the words of one commentator, of experiencing astonishment at anything.

In large part this lack of sympathy derives from the very function of religion as a means of binding together a community in the same way that a language establishes a common core of communication between individual human beings; because we do not share in the Egyptian religion any more than we share in the ancient Egyptian language, we begin automatically from the outside, looking in on a society with which we cannot, at least at first, communicate. Furthermore, failure to establish links of any kind becomes almost inevitable if we insist on approaching Egyptian beliefs and practices through the sphere that we ourselves label religion. We ought to ask ourselves at the outset what we mean by this approach, what we understand in the word religion. To say that religion is a means of communication, of allowing people to understand one another, is not enough to single it out from all other social systems of communication by speech or action. The distinctive feature of religion as a binding mechanism is that it concerns creation and, usually, a

2 Clay vulture and ram's head. Since the goddess Mut could be represented as a vulture and the god Amun as a ram, it seems likely that these figures were deposited as ex-votos in the sanctuaries of those two deities. 19th Dynasty, $c.$1250 BC; from Abydos. H. of ram's head 6.5 cm. EA 61670 and 61915.

creator or creators. The many different ways of expressing relations between the human species and the universe in which it exists are so many different sets of ideas about the great imponderables of human existence, principally the question of why we exist. While these sets of ideas need not impinge on more than a fraction of our lives, they may also be formulated as systems of thinking that we term philosophies. When a way of understanding the world is accepted and promoted by a community it ceases to be a personal philosophy and begins to affect social customs becoming, in other words, a religion. Thus religion serves two functions in society, both answering personal dilemmas concerning the nature of the world, and binding a community together. The issue of personal belief becomes submerged in the practices of the entire society in which the individual lives; only at times of great social change does the calm binding force of a religion yield to a mass movement built out of the personal doubts and faiths that we all experience at different moments.

This book will not then seek to find out 'if the Egyptians really believed in their gods and goddesses' or 'if the Egyptians were cynically manipulated by the priests', as two popular modern questions run, because if religion is regarded in this sense neither question has any meaning. Instead it investigates the ideas about creation that were endorsed and promoted by society in ancient Egypt as the binding ideas for itself, for it is possible to recognise the social character of such ideas, in other words to identify them as 'religious', from the concrete forms that they take in word and deed, providing of course that those words and deeds have left some traces in our imperfect record of the distant past.

In the case of ancient Egypt we are blessed by the natural accident of perfect geographical and climatic conditions for preserving the past. Egypt is a desert land through which the river Nile runs as the sole densely inhabitable strip, providing fresh water and fertile silt to sustain plant and animal life. The human communities in the Nile had access in the nearest deserts to a rich variety of stones for art and architecture, and the arid air has until recently protected both these and the artefacts made from organic materials such as wood, animal skins and plant fibres. The accident of nature is compounded by the equally important assistance of what we call culture, in other words lifestyle; the Egyptians buried their dead in the dry desert to offset putrefaction, and from the Neolithic to the beginning of the Christian period they included in the burials goods for the sustenance and continued existence of the deceased. This social practice varied in detail from one period to another, building up for us a wide range of study material; in the Neolithic period pottery and jewellery were already being placed in the grave, in the late Old and early Middle Kingdoms wooden models of servants on estates were sealed in the tomb, while luxury household utensils and furnishings took their place in the early New Kingdom.

Art, architecture and funerary goods have been supplemented to an increasing degree by evidence from settlement sites, where modern methods in archaeology allow the retrieval of previously unimaginable details of the ancient world; greater care in excavating and most importantly in recording finds has enabled archaeologists in Egypt to reconstruct patterns of living and behaving that round off and often correct the picture obtained from the more conventional sources of art and tomb discoveries. Inevitably there is still a bias within Egyptology for textual and pictorial evidence, because it survives from such early periods and in such remarkable quantity, even if it falls silent in many periods on such crucial areas of ancient Egyptian life as the economy or marriage. My own training is in the reading of texts rather than in excavating techniques, and this book is consequently weighted more toward texts than toward archaeological contexts of material; to correct the imbalance I would emphasise the importance of the context of each object, including objects bearing texts, and acknowledge the gaps that perforate the surviving record. Each architectural element, each work of art voices only part of a more complex whole, and can be appreciated only if its original surroundings are brought to mind; each mention of a deity in a text, each representation in two or three dimensions equally demands that attention be paid to the particular circumstances that brought the source into being. Only when the sources are respected in this way can a historian obey the rule of accuracy.

It is worth describing the different types of source and the periods at which each type occurs, to allow the reader some notion of the ground upon which this image of ancient Egyptian religion is being built up. The texts referring to deities are in the first instances personal names that include the name of a deity, such as Samut 'son of Mut' or Padiamun 'the man given by Amun'. Such names may appear limited material but they are doubly valuable because they span the full range of Pharaonic civilisation from the appearance of writing $c.$ 3000 BC to the advent of Christianity in the second and third centuries AD, and because they dent a common notion in modern studies that personal links to deities were not widely experienced until the mid-fourteenth century BC. Alongside many names appear titles, again from the earliest to the latest periods of use of hieroglyphs, and these titles too can reveal the hierarchies of temple service and, to some extent, the role of the temple in the administration as a whole, by comparing titles which refer to temples or gods with titles that do not. During the formative years between unification $c.$ 3000 BC and the Pyramid Age beginning $c.$ 2650 BC, inscriptions for the benefit of the deceased grew to longer lists of titles and to offering formulae in which material goods were requested from the offerings given by the king to the cult of deities. Offering formulae of all ages down to the Roman Period provide information on which deities were prominent above all in the funerary domain, and also gradually expanded to record in chronological order the main annual feasts at which the deceased might hope to share in offerings. With the Pyramid Age, tomb inscriptions for courtiers began to include autobiographical data and self-justifications of the owner; the latter originated as assurances that the tomb had been built on fresh ground and that its constructors had been properly recompensed, but then became texts to justify not the tomb but its owner. The self-justifications contain stock catalogues of virtues rather than autobiographical data, and so convey to us the social values of the sector and period that produced them.

Names, titles, offering formulae and 'autobiographies' all hold a particular value because they span the full range of periods and so afford a chance to compare like sources with like. The same is true of certain classes of art and architecture, such as the tomb statue, stela, burial goods, tomb-chapel and burial chamber, and above all the coffin and the items placed on the body. Architectural features in settlement sites are less well represented across all periods, although new research at sites such as Elephantine does allow a continuous history spanning all epochs in some cult centres. House chapels and religious material from domestic contexts have also not been adequately retrieved until recently. The same uneven record is true of some classes of text. Legal papyri referring to temples are rare before the seventh century BC, except among Ramesside documents; oracle texts form a special group but none are known before $c.$ 1450 BC. Letters are useful, since they record information conveyed between individuals and as well as personal observations include epistolary formulae that sometimes reveal the dominant attitudes of the age; they survive from the second millennium and, to a lesser extent, first millennium BC.

Royal funerary texts are known only from the late third, late second, and early first millennia BC, and non-royal funerary texts are found from $c.$ 2200 BC to the

3 Painted wooden stela of Amun Nakhtefmut, a god's father, shown with his daughter Shepenaset and adoring Ra-Horakhty. In the first millennium BC at Thebes such stelae were placed in the burial chamber with the coffin and the dry air and ground of the cemetery have preserved both the wood and the mineral pigments. Third Intermediate Period, $c.$ 900 BC; from Thebes. H. 27.5 cm. EA 37899.

37899

second century AD but with substantial breaks in $c.$ 1800–1600, 850–650 and 500–400 BC. These funerary manuscripts and inscriptions carry especial weight in the surviving record because, although included in the burial for the purpose of protecting the deceased and securing a perfect life after death, they were not all composed for that purpose; they include texts of incantations for warding off serpents and scorpions, of hymns, litanies and other liturgical texts, and in some cases episodes that took place between deities or at and before creation itself. Literature in a few instances presents narratives in which one or more deities take part in the action, but it is not recorded or at least does not survive except in the periods $c.$ 1850–1700, 1600–900, and 400 BC–AD 300. Literary tales help to explain or confirm short references in other sources such as tomb-chapel inscriptions, but may be tailored to the purposes of narrative rather than aiming at a strict record of the regular account of relations between deities. For example the literary *Tale of Horus and Seth* may preserve for us a large number of episodes in the struggles between those two gods in the chronological sequence that we imagine necessary for such tales; yet it is possible that some episodes have been added or modified for dramatic or other literary effect. It seems too from other sources that the episodes were in a sense self-sufficient, much as events in the Christian Gospels can be read to some extent in a different order and have a self-sufficiency that allows the Christmas story, the story of Lent and the Easter story to be read again each year; the pattern does not conflict with the life cycle of birth, growth and death but still allows each event timeless relevance to any given moment.

Temple inscriptions and statuary are also less constantly represented than the popular cliché of a society dominated by temples might have us suppose. Colossal figures of an ithyphallic god survive in the precinct of the temple of Min at Coptos as rare examples of late fourth-millennium statues of deities; early third-millennium BC votive objects from a temple deposit at Hieraconpolis include small sculptures and reliefs but these may have been placed originally in the great enclosure which was probably intended for the royal cult set up by king Khasek-hem(wy) rather than in the local temple of Horus itself. Other third-millennium examples also come from complexes dedicated not to the cult of gods but to that of the reigning king until the late third millennium when royal statues appear at a number of cult centres remote from the Residence and the pyramid complex of the king. Middle Kingdom statues of deities from temple sites survive but production of the largest statues of deities is confined to the fourteenth to twelfth and seventh to third centuries BC. Inscriptions in temples depended equally on royal patronage, and do not survive in quantity before the New Kingdom. Temple libraries were the ancient repositories of Egyptian representations and texts of the world of gods, but

4 Statue of Isis with winged arms stretched out and around Osiris as protection. This is a fine instance of large-scale sculpture of deities from the Late Period. The sculpture was donated by Sheshonq, chief steward of the 'god's wife' Ankhnesneferibra. 26th Dynasty, $c.$ 550 BC; schist, from the temple of Amun at Karnak, Thebes. H. 81 cm. EA 1162.

little survives from before the Ptolemaic Period other than by inclusion in funerary texts. Rare exceptions are items that were taken over for private use at or before burial, such as the liturgical papyri buried with an unknown Middle Kingdom lector-priest, or those placed in a family tomb in the settlement of royal craftsmen on the West Bank at Thebes, or – again at Thebes – the selection of ritual texts adopted by a priest called Nesmin in the late fourth century BC. The most substantial survivors of the wholesale destruction of temple libraries by time are the great temples in Upper Egypt at Philae, Kom Ombo, Edfu, Esna and Dendera; by having knowledge inscribed on the stone walls of those colossal undertakings the temple scribes ensured the survival of a great mass of data that has still to be adequately recorded and digested by modern scholars.

Together the texts, representations and evidence for cult and offering in practice can be assembled for each deity to build up a case study of the history of every member of the ancient pantheon. It is easy to become lost in the mass of data, and to allow the forest of detail to obscure general views and even to confirm old prejudices. The intention of this book is to fight such prejudices and to draw a more general sketch of Egyptian gods and goddesses.

The general principles of two- and three-dimensional representation in Egyptian art provide an answer to some of the deepest misconceptions and misplaced reactions in the modern experience of ancient Egypt. If we cannot recognise the principles of representation, we lose our grip on the larger and – on the personal aesthetic side – most important portion of our evidence. A widespread misconception has it that the Egyptians worshipped both dead idols and living animals. This usually provokes a reaction of disgust in a modern audience though it can be held that this demonstrates the bond felt by the Egyptians with their natural environment. The evidence giving rise to this misconception lies in the use by the Egyptians of animals and birds to represent deities, in the nurturing of a sacred animal at certain cult centres as the herald of the relevant deity (the most famous example is the Apis bull of Ptah at Memphis), and the practice of mummifying literally millions of dead animals and birds and burying them in catacombs up and down the country. Further support for the idea that the Egyptians worshipped animals with unusual fervour comes from the ancient Greek and Roman writers who recorded incidents such as the murder of a foreigner for kicking an animal, and who gave vent in some cases to their fullest powers of mockery in attacking the Egyptian deities that had the forms of animals, birds or hybrid mixes of animal and human.

5, 6 and 7 The different possibilities of representing a single deity can be seen in three contemporary images of the goddess Meresger, protectress of the Theban cemeteries. As befits the guardian of a snake-infested desert terrain, the goddess could be represented as a serpent, as in the limestone flake or ostracon of Khnummose (ABOVE), but a composition involving the goddess on a throne required that she take human shape, as in the stela of Amennakht (LEFT). On the third item the artist has combined human and animal form, placing the human head on the serpent body (RIGHT). 19th Dynasty, $c.$ 1200 BC. ABOVE Limestone. H. 16.5 cm. EA 8510. LEFT Limestone. H. 20 cm. EA 374. RIGHT Limestone. H 22.5 cm. EA 371. All from Deir el-Medina, Thebes.

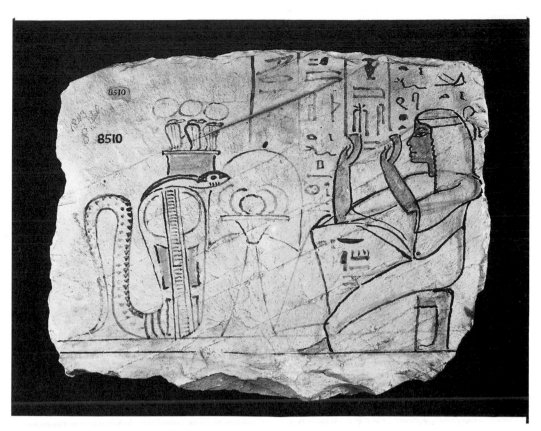

The basis for all these misconceptions is the ancient Egyptian system of representation. In Egyptian art the human form is cast in an ideal youthful condition with no emotional content other than a general serenity; representations of old age and disease are extremely rare, and even children have the proportions of adults, distinguished only by relative smaller size and a sidelock of hair. In this system of harmonious proportions and serene composition emotion can be expressed only by a dramatic recourse to an external non-human stock of symbolism. This the Egyptians took from their observation of their environment, the animal and bird life of the Nile Valley. For certain positions an animal or bird suits the shape of composition and does not produce any form that the Egyptians would find disturbing to their sense of harmony; the vulture with wings outstretched above the king, or the crocodile or jackal upon a shrine provide acceptable elements within a wider scene, as does the falcon in the specific role of title upon the rectangular frame containing the Horus-name of the king. In other contexts a pure animal or bird form would endanger the balance of a composition, most obviously when animals and birds of different sizes had to appear beside one another or when they were given human postures such as holding weaponry or insignia or sitting on thrones or embracing the king. Here the Egyptian artist employed the simple device of dividing head and body; the head identifies the deity and the body was adapted to the attribute. Thus Ra enthroned becomes a human figure, able to sit and to hold sceptres, but with a falcon head to identify him as a deity of celestial power. By the same principle the sphinx shows the king, identified by the human head with royal headcloth, but with the body of a lion to represent leonine strength. In none of these artistic conventions, however powerful they may be, is there any suggestion that the Egyptians felt affection for the animal and bird life that they were using to represent concentrated emotions, any more than the superb Neo-Assyrian reliefs of lions in lion-hunts suggest greater sympathy for the animal than for the hunter.

A stronger case for animal worship might be seen in the selection of a specially marked animal to stand as representative of a deity on earth, to be housed and fed, and to be given a lavish burial. The Mnevis bull of Ra at Iunu, the Apis bull of Ptah at Memphis and the Buchis bull of Mont at Armant are the three most famous cases of such sacred animals. It is true that these animals were given lives of luxury, were provided with food offerings, and that ceremonies were performed for their accessions and funerals; yet they were not divine in themselves as animals, but rather they fulfilled the function of making a deity tangible on earth, heralds that could be nourished and served in an indirect service of the principal deity, whether Ra, Ptah or Mont. In the case of the great animal catacombs with millions of mummified dogs, cats, ibis, fish, baboons and many other species, there are more fundamental objections to the notion that these are evidence of animal worship; in the first place, the practice of mummifying animals, birds and fish on a large scale dates to a restricted period, from the sixth century BC to about the second century AD, and secondly, recent analysis of cat mummies shows that they are all of two specific ages (kittens and two-year-olds) and that their necks are broken. Whatever the motive behind the staggering increase in mummification of animals, personal attachment seems not to have played a part.

A further area that provokes confusion in modern eyes is the tendency of Egyptian deities to fission and to fuse, for we often have the mistaken notion that each Egyptian deity should be understood as a person. If the gods and goddesses did have the rounded full characters of men and women it would be difficult to conceive of the continual mergers and internal divisions that allow the three simultaneous deities Amun, Ra and Amun-Ra, or equally the simultaneous existence of Khons alongside Khons-the-child and Khons-in-Thebes. The character of an Egyptian deity is much more that of a name that seeks to delineate an area of reference in a little-known world, in which the area delineated – in other words the area of interest to the speaker – may overlap with other areas without replacing them. Thus it is possible to appreciate the hiddenness of divinity simply as Amun 'the hidden', and it is possible for the Egyptian to appreciate divinity in the power and light of the sun simply as Ra 'the sun'; if the Egyptian wishes to combine in his approach to the godhead both ever-present invisible power and radiant heat and light, then it is possible to pronounce this third way of specifying god in the formula Amun-Ra. This fusing or merging is called syncretism by Egyptologists, and the compound deities syncretistic; their existence is in part a reflection of the long history of Pharaonic Egypt, three thousand years in which ideas have time to evolve and merge, but it is more fundamentally a part of the Egyptian practice of expressing divinity in the form of names that outline the area of concern, the area from which they seek an answer or a partner in life. The deities thus tell us what areas concerned the Egyptians, what captured their attention from one age to the next.

The same principle applies to the opposite tendency to that of syncretism, the tendency to split a named sphere into smaller units such as Horus into Horus-the-elder and Horus-the-child and Horus-in-the-horizon; as with merging into larger groups, the fissioning into smaller sections tells us that the Egyptians were adapting their area of interest. Horus covers the general area of power in the sky, but Horus-the-child is specifically the potential that is still weak and defenceless as a child, the power that needs to be nurtured; Horus-in-the-horizon is the celestial power perceived at the horizon, the break of day or the sunset. The latter focus of interest can be combined with Ra in the formula Ra-Horakhty 'the sun – the celestial power that is of the horizon', or it can be isolated as Horemakhet 'the celestial power that is in the horizon'. The example of the Horus of or in the horizon demonstrates that, although theoretically any combination or qualification is possible, only certain forms were actually adopted in ancient usage, and these were quite specifically fixed; the combination of Ra and Horus gives a regular Ra-Horakhty, and not Ra-Horemakhet, and conversely the deity of power at the horizon is in isolation regularly Horemakhet and not Horakhty. Such apparently trivial distinctions allowed the Egyptians to separate even the overlapping areas of concern that they identified for worship, and guard the modern researcher against overlooking details in naming or, on the visual side, the equally important details of iconography. By avoiding the temptation to see each deity as a fixed frame of flesh and blood we may better be able to learn from them what concerned the ancient Egyptians across the three thousand years of their civilisation.

8 Plaque with a depiction of Khons-in-Thebes wearing the sidelock of youth and a crescent moon and disk and holding a crook, flail and a composite sceptre combining the hieroglyphs for life, stability and power. The text on the right further identifies the god as 'Horus lord of joy in Ipetsut (= Karnak), Shu in Thebes', making the image an expression both of the fissioning of a deity into narrower terms of reference (Khons > Khons-in-Thebes) and of the fusion of deities with one another (Khons perceived as Horus and Shu). The name of the person for whom this plaque was carved is lost in the break at bottom right. Late Period, after 600 BC; limestone, from Thebes (?). H. 18 cm. EA 29557.

In the attempts to avoid prejudices a variety of paths to understanding appear open, from the poetical to the philosophical to the artistic, but not, paradoxically, the religious. Our expectation of what a religion should be, what a polytheistic religion is or is not, how a god and especially the creator should be represented, all stand in the way of some appreciation of the ancient Egyptian manner of relating to the universe. The European tradition rests heavily on three pillars, none of which offers a favourable hearing to Pharaonic civilisation: the Bible, in which Egypt takes the role of oppressor, classical Greece and Rome, where Egypt is viewed as a barbarian and often suspect land, and the northern, Celtic and Slavonic world with which Egypt never had any contact at all. As if this catalogue of exclusion were not enough, religion itself has ceased in European lands to function as a binding force; religions cross national boundaries and are not confined to one land, and the nation-state now enjoys other means of uniting its inhabitants, leaving the individual to organise her or his own response to existence. It may be easier to approach the ancient texts, images and objects produced by the Egyptians if we consider them on the level of what we regard as art, poetry and philosophy. We are not being asked to believe what the Egyptians may have believed, and indeed the concluding section of this book examines how very different Egyptian gods and goddesses became when they arrived on foreign shores in the Greek and Roman worlds. Instead we should try to understand, free from gross prejudice, what the Egyptian legacy consists of and how it operated. The task of looking at ancient Egypt is ethnographic, it involves ourselves; Assmann has set the task of 'dismantling clichés and unveiling a broader look at the possibilities of human existence'.

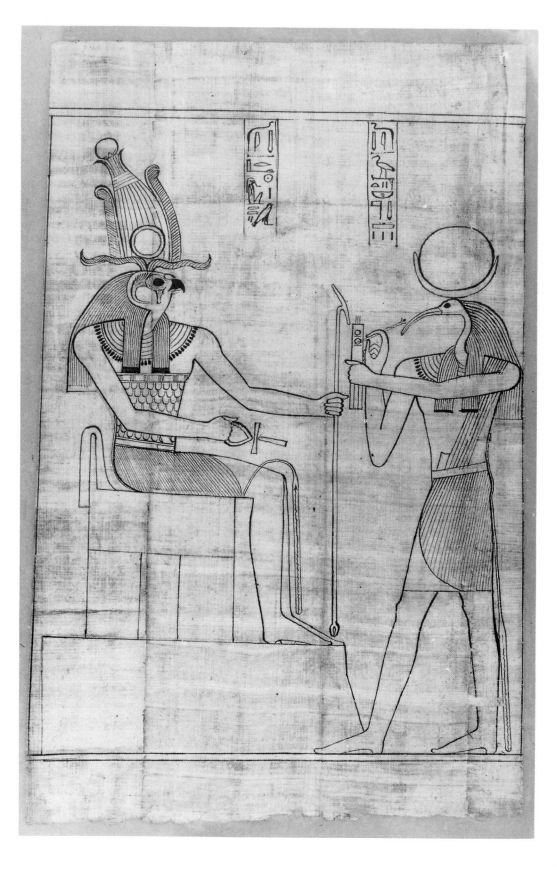

1

POWER IN HEAVEN

The Sun-god

FROM THE FIRST USE OF HIEROGLYPHS and the related system of art the Egyptians expressed an overriding appreciation for the power of the daylit sky. They found in the soaring falcon their perfect metaphor for majesty, and already the first kings took the falcon as the supreme royal title; although the name for the power embodied in this falcon was not recorded at this early stage, there is no reason to suppose that it was not Heru 'the distant one' (rendered Horus by the Greeks) as it was identified later from the Old Kingdom to the Roman Period. Yet Horus was not the only celestial power represented as a falcon; an ivory comb of the reign of Djet, of the First Dynasty, bears a motif showing the name of the king with the falcon title and, in the space immediately above, an outstretched pair of wings upon which another falcon sails in an archaic boat. The depiction presents concisely and clearly the central tenet binding together ancient Egyptian civilis-

9 ABOVE Falcon with outstretched wings, holding in each claw a plumed sceptre. Late Period, after 600 BC (?); bronze, from Thebes. W. 30 cm. EA 22840.

10 OPPOSITE Ra-Horakhty enthroned, represented as a man with falcon head wearing the *atef* crown (which comprises ram-horns and ostrich feathers) and holding the hieroglyph for life, the *ankh*, and a sceptre in the form of the hieroglyph for power. Before him stands Thoth, holding a scribal palette and reed and poised to write; he is represented with an ibis head wearing the crescent moon and disk. Third Intermediate Period, *c.*950 BC; papyrus, from Thebes. H. 48 cm. EA 10554.52.

ation, the notion that the king fulfils a role on earth under the protective wings of the celestial falcon in heaven. The boat represents movement across a large distance, automatically by boat in a land that used the river Nile for easy transport and that knew neither bridges over water nor long intercity roads (and thus had no interest in the wheel). The falcon in the celestial boat is not named, but may be assumed to denote the sun-god, since the sun is the principal heavenly body that moves across the heavens. Yet in the formative phase of Egyptian art and writing, the word *ra*, 'sun', does not seem to refer to a god; the name of one king was once read by Egyptologists as Raneb, 'Ra is my lord', but may now be interpreted as Nebra, 'lord of the sun'.

With the reign of Netjerkhet (*c.* 2650 B C) and perhaps the assistance of his chief minister Imhotep the formative years were brought to an end, through the construction of what remains among the stunning sights of the Nile Valley, the Step Pyramid at Saqqara. In place of a brick cuboid structure over the subterranean galleries of his tomb, Netjerkhet was given a mountain of stone that began in the traditional cuboid form but was transformed by the addition of upper levels into a pyramid with steps, in outline identical to the stepped podium for two thrones in kingship ceremonies. Around the Step Pyramid were laid out in stone a series of courts and halls connected with the same ceremonies, and the whole complex was enclosed in a rectangular stone enclosure wall. Although the primary focus of every feature in this complex remains the king, for whose eternal cult the buildings were designed, the pyramidal form concentrates the cult itself on lifting the king from his body in the chamber beneath the earth up to the heights of heaven. The exertion in art and architecture encouraged tighter rules of expression to govern such massive output toward the same goal. The Pyramid Age may be said to have fostered both a sharper focus on the sun and a more enduring presence in the record, thanks to the production of texts and images on a greatly increased scale in stone.

In the following century the successors of Netjerkhet modified the pyramidal form, first producing the smooth sloping sides of the true pyramid under Sneferu and then refining the angle of slope to the perfect proportions of the Great Pyramid built by Khufu, the successor of Sneferu. Around the royal pyramid the tombs of courtiers received ever more elaborate decoration in reliefs, statuary and texts, extending the range of our sources from the king to his court. From the period between Netjerkhet and Sneferu comes one of the first certain references to the sun as a god, in the name Hesyra '(he who is) praised by the sun'; the action of praising implies not an inanimate feature of the landscape but an active participant in human life, and in this name the word *ra* moves from the sense 'sun' to Ra 'sun-god'. This explicit reference to Ra inaugurates a system of relating man to the creation, a religion, in which the sun holds central place. That did not change until the Christianisation of Egypt in the late Roman Period three thousand years later.

The cult centre of the sun-god lay at a city named Iunu, known to the Greeks as Heliopolis 'city of the sun'; its close position first to Egyptian Babylon (a Roman fortress city to the south) and then Coptic and Islamic Cairo cost it virtually all of its monuments, and today a sole obelisk of Senusret I stands on the site in the Cairo suburb Matariya, near the airport where most visitors to the country now arrive. In

Pharaonic times Iunu must have contained among the most lavishly adorned sanctuaries in the land. The earliest evidence for royal patronage consists of relief fragments that date precisely to the reign of Netjerkhet, the king of the first great solar monument, the Step Pyramid. At Iunu, as elsewhere in the record, the sun-god was represented through the metaphor of the falcon, either a sun-disk with outstretched wings or a complete perching or soaring falcon. In scenes where the deity accompanied the king and others, or took human postures such as holding sceptres or sitting enthroned, the head alone was given falcon shape, to identify the deity, while the body was shown in human form, to carry the attributes of the deity. The name of the god is generally given as Ra, 'sun-god', but often combines with reference to the god embodying power over earth, Horus; in this combination Horus takes the aspect of a god of the horizon, where the power of the sun is seen in its rising and setting, and the name of the sun-god thus becomes Ra-Horakhty, 'the sun-god, the Horus of the horizon'.

The sun embodied for the Egyptians more than power in heaven or power over earth; the daily guarantee of sunrise after the sunset of yesterday offered a bright and tangible promise of resurrection, and for this reason the sun-god was considered the central and original power of creation. The existence and above all the birth of the universe present every human being with an intractable problem, to which every society finds some means of responding. Our society (not necessarily its scientists) provides a natural scientific theory in which there remains considerable uncertainty over how Newtonian physics and Einstein's relativity theory should be made to take into account the more complicated findings of new physicists. Ancient Egypt answered the same universal questions with a more tightly drawn worldview centred on the Nile Valley alone, but including powerful poetic accounts of creation that function at least as well as the vague general level of understanding of natural sciences in our own times. In Egyptian texts the sun-god as creator is named Atum, 'the All', in other words the substance from which all creation unfurled; this pre-eminence over all created matter was depicted by representing Atum in the guise of a king of Egypt, as lord of the universe, in human form wearing the Double Crown of Egypt. The origin of the world itself seems to have been not so much an act of creation in the manner of the Judaeo-Christian concept where a god creates the world in a specific period of time; rather the creator and his creation emerged spontaneously out of the void before time and before matter. One text, among the most widely copied on coffins and funerary papyri, describes the creator at the dawn of existence. Shorn of the extensive commentary interspersed through the text even in the earliest versions, it provides the following opening verse:

> Incantation for coming forth by day in the necropolis:
> the word took form, all was mine, when I existed alone;
> I am Ra in his first appearances, when he shines forth from the horizon;
> I am the great god who took form of himself, who created his names,
> lord of Enneads, who has no opponent among the gods;
> yesterday is mine, and I know tomorrow.
> (from Coffin Texts 335)

23

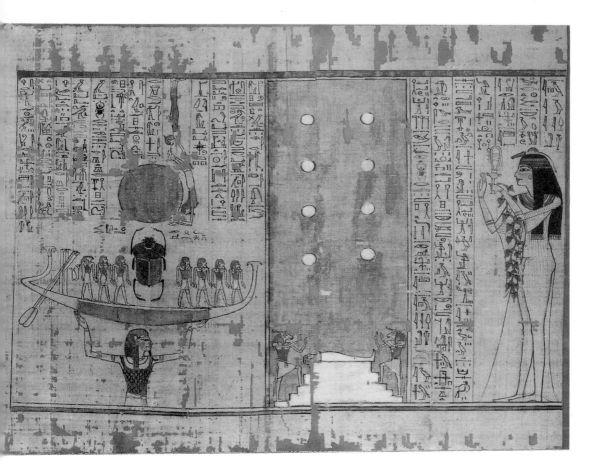

11 The left end of the *Book of the Dead* of the noblewoman Anhay, entitled chantress of Amun and shown to the right with one hand outstretched in adoration and the other holding the sistrum and a plant resembling ivy. The sun-god is shown as a beetle with the sun-disk in a boat which is lifted up by the primeval deity Nun. Above, the goddess Nut raises Osiris to receive the sun-disk into the Underworld. Between this scene and the figure of Anhay a more enigmatic motif evoking creation is depicted, in which two ram-headed men adore a mummified body resting on a stepped platform beneath eight white disks. 20th Dynasty, *c*.1150 BC; painted papyrus, from Thebes. H. 42 cm. EA 10472, part.

The value of the text for the Egyptians can be seen in the title of 'coming forth by day in the necropolis', taken up in the New Kingdom as a title for the entire corpus of funerary texts known to Egyptology as the *Book of the Dead*. The passage cited presents the creator as the original owner of all (*atum*) and identifies him as Ra, the sun, at its first rising. The theme of a world taking shape out of this primeval being is elaborated in a text known from a fourth-century BC papyrus:

Book of knowing the forms of Ra and of felling Aapep; words spoken
by the lord of the universe, which he said after he took form:
I it is who took form (kheper) as Khepri.
I took form; (other) forms took form.
All forms took form after I took form.
Forms multiplied in emerging from my mouth,
before earth existed, before sky existed, before snakes and worms were created in
that place . . .
I made all shapes alone, before I sneezed out Shu, before I spat out Tefnut, before
any other took form and had acted with me.

These texts address the central problem of 'something out of nothing' by locating the primeval sun-god within the world before matter. That world appears in these texts as an infinite expanse of dark and directionless waters, given the name Nun. In some texts the four principles of Nun are personified as male and female deities with names; exactly which principle is named varies from one text and one period to another, but invariably the principle is a characteristic opposite to characteristics of the familiar world inhabited by human beings: Amun and Amunet the male and female 'Hidden-ness' or invisibility, Hehu and Hehut the male and female 'Infinite Water' or lack of finite bounds, Tenem and Tenemet the pair for 'Straying' or lack of direction, Keku and Kekut 'Darkness' or lack of light. These deities suggest a first implicit differentiation of matter, undermining the single unbroken expanse of the primeval waters Nun; together with the fixed number of four pairs (perhaps for the four cardinal points, another breach of the infinity of Nun) the creator could form a fifth entity.

These deities were revered at the cult centre of Thoth in Middle Egypt, Ashmunein, known to the Greeks as Hermopolis, 'city of Hermes' (equated by them with Thoth); the high priest of Thoth was titled 'Leader of the Five', and the eight primeval beings gave their name to the city, in Egyptian Khemenu, 'the Eight'. The texts concerning the Eight are often called the 'Hermopolitan Theology', but this creates the perhaps erroneous impression that the different strands of belief come from different local origins and were synthesised together to form a hybrid mass of contradictory beliefs. It seems far more likely from the content of the texts that they belong together from the outset, and that different localities then put their own emphasis on particular parts of the unitary system of beliefs.

Some of the most striking accounts of the unfurling of creation survive on coffins from Bersha, a necropolis for the nobility of Ashmunein in the Middle Kingdom. The texts in question were used if not composed to enable the deceased to gain power over the element of air as part of the armoury of self-defence that would secure a good life after death. Atum spat out, sneezed or masturbated two offspring from himself; the raw physical terms simply express the mystery of fissioning, of how one being can produce from itself another without assistance. The Bersha texts explore this primeval trinity of Atum, his 'son' Shu, 'dry air', and his 'daughter' Tefnut, 'corrosive moist air', in phrasing that makes it abundantly clear that the kinship terms applied to Egyptian deities are not attempts to produce literal family genealogies for the divine world, but rather metaphors, just as representations in two or three dimensions are metaphors and not attempts to see divine beings literally as animals, birds or hybrids. The following extract illustrates this point by giving the two first products of Atum more abstract identities as life and right, two universal principles of human existence:

Then Atum said: Tefnut is my living daughter who will be with her brother Shu; life is his name, right is her name. I will live with my twins, I will live with my two fledglings, see I am amid them, one of them at my back, one in my belly.

The two life-giving principles can thus be equated with a series of different paired features. Shu embodies as dry air the force of preservation, and thus not only life itself but also the concept of time as a series of events endlessly repeated in an eternal cycle called by the Egyptians *neheh*. Tefnut is the opposite as moist and so corrosive air, and embodies the relentless rule of change and the concept of time as a series of unique events in a single line called by the Egyptians *djet*. *Neheh* is the pattern of time that we recognise in the repeated seasons of the year, or repeated cycles of movement of sun, moon and stars, while *djet* is the chronological sequence of time that we observe in the succession of individual years and individual generations. The Bersha texts illustrate the birth of time at the eve of existence.

The same text goes on to refer to the creation of mankind from the 'eye' of the creator:

> *the eye that I had sent forth when I was alone with Nun, inert,*
> *before I had found a place where I might stand or sit,*
> *before Iunu was founded in which I might exist,*
> *before the lotus had been bound on which I might sit.*

The eye provides one of the richest, most enduring and pervasive of Egyptian motifs. It relates sometimes to the creator, to Ra, sometimes to Horus, but always to the power to see, illuminate and act. It is also far from fixed, and indeed the strength of its metaphor for power depends on its ability to move; it leaves or is taken from the deity, and must be coaxed back or restored, providing a far more earnest expression of wholeness and power than if it had never moved at all. The most frequently recorded account of the eye of the sun concerns an episode after creation, but the Bersha text states explicitly that its luminous power was already active as the world was moving from an unending mass of undifferentiated matter to the divided world of human experience.

The moment of creation, of the unfurling of matter out of the primeval matters, was repeated for the Egyptians every year in an event of their natural environment, the Nile flood. Every summer the low-lying fields and marshes in the Nile Valley were returned to the condition of primordial waters as the river swelled from the summer rains at its Ethiopian and Sudanese highland sources; every autumn, as the floodwaters drained to the Mediterranean Sea, the fields would emerge not as they had been before the flood but coated in a fertile layer of new silt brought down by the river from higher up the valley to the south. In Egyptian terms each new occurrence repeated the 'first time', when the waters receded to reveal the first shallows out of which a lotus-flower could bloom to support the sun-god, and then

12 Two emblems of protective power on the sarcophagus of Pairkap; on the left a cobra with outstretched wings is swollen poised to strike, and to the right is a *wedjat* or 'eye of wholeness', a stylised representation of a human eye with the markings of a falcon head. 30th Dynasty, *c.*350 BC (?); black granite, from Cairo (original provenance Saqqara ?). EA 66, detail.

the first dry land upon which the sun-god could find solid ground to rest. The fragrant lotus took the name Nefertem and played the role of vivifying the emerging sun-god, just as the scent of the lotus revivified the Egyptians in their leisure. The ground itself was conceived as a lump of rock named the *benben*-stone, a word connected to *weben*, 'to shine', and used as the image of the pyramid, its capstone the pyramidion and the pyramidal tip of the obelisk; the sanctuary at Iunu housed the stone in a shrine called the 'house of the *benben*'. The sun-god emerged either from an egg, a transparent and evocative metaphor for new life, or as the bird named *benu*, also from the kernel of words around *weben* and resembling a heron; the *benu*-heron appears to be part of the inspiration for the classical tale of the phoenix, a fabulous bird that was born from the ashes after a fixed number of years, again carrying the message of resurrection guaranteed by the sun.

At the 'first time' the creator appears alone, but the texts cited above demonstrate that his emergence postdated an internal development by which he had already separated from the primeval waters Nun, and already enjoyed the company of Shu and Tefnut as life-creating principles. The magic spark of change that brought matter into existence could also be expressed as the female principle (female because it involves giving birth), worshipped at Iunu as a goddess in female form named Iusaas, 'she grows great as she comes'. In addition the divine eye that existed before creation could be envisaged as a goddess, the loving daughter Hathor or her raging *alter ego* Sekhmet; as the goddess Nebethetepet, 'mistress of offerings', she shared a place in the cult at Iunu. The faculty that allowed the primeval deity to develop into the existing world was also identified as Heka, a word often translated as 'magic' and which denotes the intangible energy of creative power that defends the sun-god and mankind from the forces of darkness. Heka is joined by two other forces that make creation and all action possible, Sia, 'perception', and Hu, 'pro-

27

13 ABOVE A scene from the *Book of the Dead* of Hunefer, who is shown adoring the *benu*-heron; the bird is labelled here '*ba* of Ra'. 19th Dynasty, *c*. 1285 BC; painted papyrus, from Thebes. EA 9901, detail.

14 OPPOSITE Tomb stela of Padiamennebnesuttawy, showing in the upper register the solar boat with the ram-headed sun-god, here named 'flesh of the god', accompanied by a crew including Hu, Sia and Heka. In the lower register Padiamennebnesuttawy is depicted adoring the sun-god in three separate forms, Ra-Horakhty with falcon head, Atum with the Double Crown of kingship and Khepri with a scarab-beetle on his head. Behind these solar forms are the funerary deities Osiris, Isis and Nephthys with the jackal-headed Anubis; as desert scavenger, the jackal threatened the dead and was propitiated as Anubis, necropolis god specifically of embalming. 30th Dynasty or early Ptolemaic Period, 4th to 3rd centuries BC; painted plaster on wood, from Thebes. H. 74 cm. EA 8462.

nouncement', respectively the foresight and the creative word that enable plans to be first formulated and then fulfilled.

The division of the world into dry land amid the waters implied a space above the land, in other words a sky; in Egyptian texts and representations this new division takes the guise of a development out of the existing or pre-existing principles of Life = preserving = dry air = Shu and of Right = changing = moist air = Tefnut. Thus the dry air (Shu) becomes the dry land (Geb) while moist air (Tefnut) becomes

the sky (Nut) conceived as a mirror-image of the original waters and so as a watery expanse. In family terms Shu and Tefnut give birth to Geb and Nut. The world is further divided when Geb and Nut produce four offspring, the gods of disorder, Seth, and of order, Osiris, and their sisters Nephthys and Isis. The new generation completes the number of nine deities, an Ennead, that began with the primeval creator-god. In Egyptian writing three is used to represent the plural number, and nine provides a symbolic means of denoting, as three times three, a plurality of pluralities, in other words a shorthand way of denoting 'all'. The Ennead of the sun-god is known in Egyptology as the Heliopolitan Ennead, and the texts concerning these deities as the Heliopolitan Theology but, as with the Hermopolitan Theology, the term seems to give the false impression of two once independent systems of beliefs that would supposedly have been welded together; it would be better to regard the different accounts as expressions of different emphases within a single and integral whole.

15 Figure of Sekhmet enthroned over prostrate enemies. Late Period, after 600 BC; green glazed composition, of unknown provenance. H. 19.5 cm. EA 60279.

Initially the sun-god himself ruled on earth over this creation, in which human and divine beings now existed. No text illustrates better the origin of all things in the sun-god than the *Book of the Adoration of Ra*, a composition first attested in the burial chamber of Useramun, vizier of Hatshepsut, and then in the tombs of New Kingdom kings. This litany addresses Ra in all his seventy-four forms, including alongside familiar deities such as Nun, Shu, Tefnut, Isis and Horus, other mysterious beings such as 'the Fiery One'. Exactly midway in the series comes the thirty-seventh form 'the Boar', locating at the heart of creation the omnivorous appetite that otherwise excluded the pig from religious contexts. Each form is shown mummified, in other words potent with new life, and for each a short verse of adoration is recorded, as may be illustrated from the text for the form Nephthys: 'Praise to you Ra, tall of power, whose head shines for what is in front of him; you are the corpse of Nephthys'. The sun-god is at the same time the substance of all things and their creator.

The account of the departure of the sun-god from the world to the heavens survives only from copies that date to the restoration of traditional religion after the reign of Akhenaten, and may be somewhat modified by the momentous changes of that period. Nevertheless they provide a clear version of the fall of humanity from divine grace, an episode that would otherwise remain confined to obscure references in other texts. The account describes the reaction of the sovereign Ra to a human rebellion; he sends out his eye to slaughter the rebels, a deed that it accomplishes as Sekhmet 'the Powerful', raging fury, to return contented as Hathor, the motherly cow and loving mistress. Sekhmet revels in an ecstasy of slaughter and to prevent it continuing Ra resorted to deception; he had red ochre added to seven thousand jugs of beer to make it look like human blood, and when the goddess drank the brew her rage turned to drunken sweetness and she ceased to destroy. The two goddesses, raging Sekhmet and content Hathor, act as two sides of the same nature, extreme expressions of a single passion, the rage that can be coaxed back to placidity, or the love that turns to hate. Fury is expressed in Pharaonic art as a lion, embodying the power to destroy enemies, and a range of protective goddesses were represented in this form. Although modern onlookers are often baffled by the use of the same imagery for different deities (that is, different names of deities), image and name combine in every instance to form a differently nuanced expression of one central theme, the protective power of dangerous force.

The goddess of protective ointment Bast ('she of the *bas*, ointment-jar') originally took leonine form, until the first millennium B C when she was shown instead as a cat, a creature more clearly ambivalent, able to switch from purring contentment to savage attack. Tefnut, as first daughter of Ra and the equivalent of Right, took the leonine form, and appeared in a late version of the story as the goddess-eye who had to be coaxed back to Ra from Nubia; the southern connection gave this story a particular force in the Late Period when kings from what is now the Sudan conquered Egypt and renewed many ancient textual and artistic traditions. Other goddesses to be represented as lionesses included Wadjyt, a goddess more typically depicted in the form of a cobra, which could be portrayed head raised and swollen

16 LEFT Figure of Bast wearing the Double Crown of kingship and suckling a king who holds the crook. Third Intermediate Period, $c.$ 800 BC; blue glazed composition, of unknown provenance. H. 7 cm. EA 11314.

17 OPPOSITE Figure of a cat, the animal used to represent the goddess Bast. Late Period, after 600 BC; hollow cast copper alloy inlaid with gold, of unknown provenance. H. 8.2 cm. EA 22927.

at the brow of the king, to spit fiery venom at his enemies. The cobra on the forehead of the sovereign was called in Egyptian *iaret*, 'the rising goddess', or *nesret*, 'the fiery goddess'. A third protective goddess in royal iconography was the vulture, shown flying behind the king with wings outstretched; the vulture was incorporated into the crown of the queen, as the woman appointed to escort the king, earthly manifestation of the sun-god. As the counterpart to the cobra Wadjyt, the vulture was named as Nekhbet, 'she of Elkab', and the two goddesses appointed to the opposite ends of the Two Lands of Egypt, Wadjyt to Buto in the Delta and Nekhbet to Elkab in southern Upper Egypt. The goddess Mut, consort of Amun in the New Kingdom and later, drew on the imagery of both vulture and lioness, but stood more often as a woman, as did Hathor when representing human sexual love.

The intermediary in the shift between the emotions of rage and peace was identified as the god Thoth and portrayed either as an ibis or baboon. As the lesser companion to the sun, Thoth was considered god of the moon, and his homage to the more powerful solar deity found an echo in the noisy chatter of baboons at dawn when the first light from the sun brought the world to life every day anew. Perhaps because the phases of the moon have been used to calculate fractions of time, and provide a celestial example of a whole becoming by degrees less and then greater again, the moon-god Thoth became god of knowledge, not least written knowledge, as well as the deity that brought the message of the sun-god to his daughter the eye and then returned her to her father. In one funerary text of the Middle Kingdom Thoth declares, 'I have pacified the Fiery Goddess, and have raised Right to the one who loves her [i.e. the sun-god]'. In the Late Period tale of Tefnut as the distant eye-goddess, it is Thoth who coaxes her back out of Nubia. The task of bringing the eye back to Ra, of raising Right to the creator, was equivalent to healing creation, and the image of Thoth as a baboon offering the *wedjat*, 'eye of wholeness', came to be considered an expression of both cult and kingship; all cult involved maintaining what is right and orderly, and kingship was

18 Plaque with a representation of Thoth as a baboon offering the *wedjat*-eye to Ra, depicted as the winged sun-disk. Ptolemaic Period, 3rd century BC or later; limestone, of unknown provenance. H. 36 cm. EA 1425.

19 OPPOSITE Representation of Nut as the sky arched over an ithyphallic figure of Geb as the earth, from the vignette papyrus of Tameniu. Third Intermediate Period, *c.*950 BC; painted papyrus, from Thebes. H. (as cut and framed today) 9.5 cm. EA 10008.

the mainstay both of the cult of the gods and of their world. In Ptolemaic and Roman temples the offering of Right became one of the commonest scenes depicted on temple walls, and the eye-offering baboon became a hieroglyph for the Egyptian word for king, *nesut*, reinterpreted as *in-su*, 'its bringer'. The task also found expression as a separate deity Inheret, 'the god who brings back the distant one', later venerated at the hometown of the First Dynasty, Tjeni (Greek Thinis) in the area of Abydos.

Despite the victory of his eye over the rebels Ra resolved to leave the earth and ordered Nut to make herself distant from the earth as the sky, lifted aloft by Shu and the eight gods termed Heh, 'infinite'. The sun-god now took a boat to traverse the skies, and the seamless flow of light and time became divided into the hours of the day and night. The universe thus consisted for the Egyptians of an eternal process, a cycle of light and darkness, occupying the restricted space of Geb, Shu and Nut (earth, air and sky) in the middle of the open expanses of Nun, the primeval waters, like an air bubble within a limitless ocean. The journey of the sun through the day sky to rest in the evening and through the night sky to be born in the morning gave the universe the character of perpetual motion, as distinct from the static view of the world common to classical Greek, Roman and Judaeo-Christian concepts of the cosmos. The Egyptians, in their meticulous observation of their environment, perceived in the scarab or dung-beetle pushing a ball of dung the pattern of the sun-disk propelled across the sky, and the scarab thus became a

symbol of solar regeneration as Khepri, the sun-god who takes visible shape in the morning sky. *Kheper*, 'to take shape', also provided the name of the beetle, *kheprer*.

The process never freed itself from the risk of collapse, the danger that the forces of disintegration would engulf the bark of the sun, and this threat was pictured by the Egyptians in the form of the serpent Aapep on whose coils Ra might founder like a boat on a sandbank in the Nile. Each hour contained obstacles and so each was ascribed a protective deity, such as Maat, 'Right', for the first hour of day. The cyclical repetition of events, *neheh*, mirrored but never captured the perfection of the first time, the rule of the sun-god on earth, because following the rebellion of mankind there was now Wrong in the world. In two texts the sun-god is justified against the existence of evil by describing his good deeds. In the first, from a literary text known as the *Instruction for king Merykara* the creator-god is said to act for humanity:

> *He makes daylight for their hearts,*
> *he journeys that they might see ...*
> *when they weep, he hears.*
> *He has made for them a ruler in the egg,*
> *a protector to protect at the back of the weak-armed.*
> *He has made for them* heka-*power as a weapon to repel the arm of events,*
> *watchful over them as by day, so by night.*

The second passage is placed in the very mouth of the creator and defends him against the charge of uncaring negligence more forcefully; it is recorded as a funerary text on coffins from Bersha.

Words spoken by the secret-of-names, the lord of the universe ... I have carried out four good deeds within the portal of the horizon. I made the four winds, that every person might breathe in his time: that is one of the deeds. I made the great flood, that the poor might be mighty like the rich: that is one of the deeds. I made every man like his fellow; I did not ordain that they do evil, it is their hearts that destroyed what I had said: that is one of the deeds. I made their hearts not forget the West (where the dead were buried), from the wish that divine offerings be made to the local deities: that is one of the deeds.

Though the sun-god was thus absolved of creating the evil in the world, he was faced with the need to ward off attack just like any other creature in this precarious creation. The cosmic journey could only avoid coming to a standstill if it was constantly supported by cult and justice, and to this end the sun-god installed a king on earth to act as his successor. In the generations of the first deities the kingship passed from Ra to Shu to Geb to Osiris (under whom the story takes a violent turn as explored in the next chapter). In human experience the place of the sun-god was filled on earth by the king, who was not a mortal human being but a mortal god sharing in the same substance as the sun-god.

The divine birth of the king formed part of the core of belief taken for granted and therefore it was not recorded until Hatshepsut whose right to rule was in doubt because she was a woman claiming to take the male role of the male sun-god. The narrative is echoed once in a late Middle Kingdom tale about a change in ruling

20 Cylinder seal inscribed with the name Merytra, the chief name (Horus-name) of the king Sobekneferu. She was the first known woman to claim kingship over Egypt. Her title is expressed graphically as 'the female Horus', a falcon with the feminine ending t (a small semicircular sign representing a loaf), and is written in place of the falcon alone above the rectangular frame in which the Horus-name appeared. The Horus-name Merytra also declares the presence of a woman on the throne of Horus, for it means 'she who is beloved of Ra'. Hatshepsut was the next woman to claim kingship, three hundred years after Sobekneferu. Whereas Hatshepsut built extensively at Thebes, where monuments have survived relatively well, Sobekneferu seems to have focused on the area of Memphis and the Fayum, where stone has been quarried for use in more recent cities in the vicinity. As a result, only fragments of her monuments survive and it is not even known whether she ever reigned alone or always shared the throne with a man, as Hatshepsut did with Thutmose III. 12th Dynasty, $c.$ 1800 BC; glazed steatite, of unknown provenance. H. 5 cm. EA 16581.

family, and after Hatshepsut it was used in the temple of Amenhotep III at Luxor, apparently dedicated to the mystery of divine (pro-)creation. In the fourth century BC and later the great building projects in Upper Egypt included structures now termed birth-houses where the birth of the divine child was celebrated.

The narrative of divine birth begins with the selection of a human woman to hold the seed of the sun-god; he impregnates the mother by taking the guise of her human spouse. It is irrelevant to the story whether the human parents are the reigning king and his queen, because their role is that of surrogate parents to provide a home on earth for the offspring of the sun-god. The woman is told by Thoth, herald of the gods, that she is to give birth to the next son of the sun-god; the child is fashioned by the god Khnum with its *ka* or sustaining spirit, a deed portrayed as the moulding of two small figures on a potter's wheel. The birth itself is assisted by a host of divine beings. Although the tale is known only from relatively late sources, the royal title 'son of Ra' appears in the age of the building of the Giza pyramids $c.$ 2600 BC, and is in keeping with the strong solar emphasis that began at that time. The literal belief in the king as the stuff of the sun-god can be seen equally clearly in a Middle Kingdom description of the death of the king, from the literary text that Egyptologists call the *Tale of Sanehat* (or, from Coptic spellings of the words, Sinuhe); 'the god ascended to his horizon, the dual king Sehetepibra (the throne name of Amenemhat I), he rose up to the sky and united with the sun-disk, the divine body merging with its maker'.

Once created the king was predestined for the throne of his heavenly father, and his duties are succinctly delineated in one of the most extraordinary compositions to survive from Pharaonic Egypt, highlighted by the Egyptologist Jan Assmann who has named the text the *King as Priest of the Sun*. The text provides a description of kingship to accompany the liturgy of hymns to the sun performed by the king at key moments in the daily solar cycle, and for this reason it was inscribed on the walls of chambers linked to that aspect of cult, such as the solar shrine in the temple of Hatshepsut at Deir el-Bahri. It was even taken over for private use on one Ramesside papyrus as an introduction to a hymn to the sun, in a *Book of the Dead*

37

now in the British Museum. From the eleven examples known Assmann has reconstructed the complete text in which one passage relates to the nature of kingship most directly:

Ra has placed the king on the earth of the living for ever and eternity to judge humanity and to pacify the gods, to realise Right and to annihilate Wrong; he gives divine offerings to the gods, funerary offerings to the transfigured dead, the name of the king is in the sky like that of Ra, he lives in elation like Ra-Horakhty'.

This account does not add up to a complete description of the early state, which royal annals portray more as an organism that acquires costly commodities by trade, direct mining and quarrying and warfare, and then expends them in court and cult activity such as the production of statues and making of offerings. Yet it does embrace the balance of cult and justice that the king was expected to uphold; the world was ruled by partnership of the sun as *netjer aa*, 'great god' or 'senior partner', and the king, *netjer nefer* '(youthfully) perfect god' or 'junior partner'. The king ruled 'all that the sun encircles' and his sovereignty was expressed as a circuit extended to an oval in which to write his birth and throne-names.

Ra was a visible sovereign, as the sun-disk in the sky, but from the Middle Kingdom he was joined by a complement to express a concept more familiar to

21 Statue pedestal inscribed with the Horus-name and cartouches of Ramses II either side of two cartouches each with the name of queen Merytamun; all four cartouches rest on the hieroglyph for gold, symbolising eternity. Although the cartouche marked above all the sovereignty of the reigning king, it was occasionally extended to women in the royal family to express their role of escort to the representative of the sovereign sun on earth. 19th Dynasty, *c*.1250 BC; black granite, of unknown provenance. W. 52.7 cm. EA 1662.

Judaism, Christianity and Islam, the invisible divinity that is present unseen everywhere in the world; this complement was Amun 'the hidden one'. In the Old Kingdom Amun appears only as one of the pre-existent aspects of nothingness, an opposite of the world of matter, like Keku, 'darkness'. His obscurity ends from the time that the rulers of Thebes began to claim the kingship of the Two Lands in c. 2000 B C; the local governor Intef set up a monument from which one octagonal column survives, reused in the foundations of a later construction, and one face of the column bears above the royal titles and name Intef the identity of the new deity 'Amun-Ra, lord of the sky, power of the land, pillar of the fighting(?)-province'. As the 'hidden' invisible divine power Amun provided the ideal cipher for the burgeoning ambitions of the Theban rulers. As a universal force Amun could be conceived in Egyptian terms as an aspect of Ra, in the compound form Amun-Ra, and this deity became the principal god of empire in the New Kingdom, when Egypt controlled the goldmines of Nubia and trade-routes of Syria-Palestine. Under the Tuthmosside kings the treasuries of Amun in his main temple at Karnak filled with the spoils of war and the gains of international trade, and the cult centre grew throughout the following millennium to become the largest religious complex on earth.

Although the temples, as examined in chapter three, did not stand outside royal control but functioned as branches of the national administration, the god Amun and his cult created at Thebes a unique counterpart to the rule of the king. Thebes lay far from the centre of power at Memphis or farther north in the Delta, where Ramses II established his capital Per-Ramses, 'domain of Ramses'. In the absence of the king the Theban temples and the Theban god Amun took on the role of administration and ruler in southern Upper Egypt. The adoration of the sun faced two virtual rivals, the divine king and the royal god, and at Thebes the king appeared secondary to the creator both by his absence from the area other than for brief visits and by the magnificence of the royal endowments for Amun.

Political ambivalence found a match in theological rivalry between hidden omnipresent Amun and visible omnipotent Ra; hymns to the sun focus more and more on the physical aspect of the sun-disk, as in the celebrated lyric of adoration of Amun-Ra on the stela of Hor and Suty, two brothers who, beside being the only twins recorded from ancient Egypt, oversaw construction work on either side of the Nile at Thebes in the reign of Amenhotep III:

> *In a brief day you run a course of leagues in millions and hundreds of*
> *thousands; every day is a moment with you, passed by when you set, when*
> *you have completed the hours of the night likewise ...*
> *when you stir to shine forth at dawn, your radiance opens the eyes*
> *of the herd;*
> *when you set in the western horizon, then they slumber as though they were*
> *dead.*

The second hymn of the twins even begins 'hail disk of the day', identifying as the deity the sun-disk, in Egyptian *Aten*, a first indication of a radical turn in the relation between the king and the sun-god.

39

22 Stela with a representation of Amun as a man with a double-plumed crown, enthroned and receiving flowers and adoration from the royal craftsman Nebnefer. 19th Dynasty, c. 1200 BC; painted limestone, from Deir el-Medina, Thebes (?). H. 25.5. cm. EA 65336.

23 Stela with the upper register depicting Paser, the mayor of Thebes, adoring Amun, Mut his consort and Khons the divine child of the Theban triad; in the lower register appears a goddess enthroned, 'Thebes the victorious', a personification of the district of Thebes first attested in the Middle Kingdom. 20th Dynasty, c. 1150 BC; limestone, from Thebes (?). H. 42.2 cm. EA 1214.

Amenhotep III was succeeded by his son Amenhotep IV, who began early in his reign to construct a great new temple to the sun, on land east of the main temple of Amun at Karnak. In the sixth year of the reign he founded a new city in Middle Egypt, dedicating it to the sun-god as Aten and naming it Akhetaten 'horizon of Aten'. The king also transformed the style of representation to a new system of proportions that gave the human figure slenderer form with feminine hips and a thin waist, elongated chin and tall skull. The most radical departure came in the relation to all other deities; not only was the sun-god portrayed simply as a sun-disk with rays ending in hands proffering the sign of life to the royal family, but even more astonishingly the other deities were simply dropped from royal patronage. Amenhotep changed his name, which means 'Amun is content', to Akhenaten 'one beneficial to the Aten', and sent out agents to erase the name and image of Amun in every corner of the land, from the tips of obelisks to the remotest shrines in Nubia. The other deities seem not to have suffered the same persecution, although Mut and the phrase 'the gods' were often also destroyed, as were images of the inundation Hapy, a role of fertile motherhood that the king and his god reserved for themselves. The hymns to Aten build on the imagery of existing solar hymns, but in the new hymns the sun traverses the sky alone and mute. Prayer had to be channelled through the king, and shrines at home had to replace the old gods with images of the royal family under the rays of the Aten. At Akhetaten the decoration of the tombs of the nobles depicts the court bowing in uniform obeisance to the king; there is no room here for a direct relation between the individual and god, all divine contact being reserved for king and god. In the tombs of courtiers the old hymns to Ra, spoken by the tomb-owner, were replaced at Akhetaten by the royal hymn to the Aten, spoken by the king himself, except in two particularly important tomb-chapels, those of the senior courtier Ay and of Meryra the high priest of the Aten. The title of the hymn gives the name of the sun-god as a formula in two cartouches, another innovation to emphasise the partnership of king and sun-god as in a co-regency:

Adoration of the living Ra-Horakhty rejoicing in the horizon, in his name of the air (shu) which is in the sun-disk (aten); . . . when you set in the western horizon of the sky they sleep in the manner of the dead, their heads swathed, their noses stopped until you shine forth from the eastern horizon of the sky . . .
(from the shorter hymn to the Aten)

As you scatter darkness, as you cast your rays, the Two Lands are in festival . . . The entire land takes up its work, all animals content at their plants, trees and plants springing up, birds flying up from their nests, their wings praising your ka, all herds frolic afoot, all that flies off and alights, they live when you shine for them.
(from the longer hymn to the Aten)

The vision of the sun in these hymns comes close to the depiction of god in the psalms, but there is an important difference between the sun-god Aten of Akhenaten on the one hand and both the Judaeo-Christian-Islamic deity and the traditional Egyptian sun-god Ra on the other. The sun-god of Akhenaten is not engaged with humanity beyond dawning to give light and life, a task that it

24 Fragment of a stela from a household shrine at Akhetaten, showing the king Akhenaten with protruding chin and belly, under the arms of the sun-disk, itself now all but entirely destroyed at top left. 18th Dynasty, $c.$ 1325 BC; limestone, from Akhetaten (modern Amarna). H. 25 cm. EA 24431.

performs for every other living being on earth as well, animal or vegetable. The course of Aten across the sky has no moral content, and the king defends only the truth that Aten is sole god, not the moral and social order. This deficiency and the fact that access to the sun-god remained exclusively in the royal preserve may have encouraged the reversion to traditional religion as much as any political manoeuvres at court or among the leading families of the land. After the reign of Akhenaten a stela recording the restoration of the temples of Egypt proclaims that Tutankhamun, his successor, 'has expelled Wrong throughout the Two Lands, Right is firm in her place, he has caused Wrong to be abhorred, and the land to be as it was at the first time'. The traditional deities regained their positions, but the sun-god did not cease to receive the major share of adoration and to offer the most substantial promise of resurrection. One extended hymn to the sun in the Memphite tomb-chapel of Horemheb, army chief under the boy-king Tutankhamun,

43

takes care to intersperse the text with other deities, although there is no mistaking the principal godhead:

> *Adoration of Ra, pacifying him when he shines forth . . .*
> *Hail to you, the luminous, the sharp, Atum-Horakhty,*
> *as you are risen in the horizon of the sky, praises to you are in everyone's mouth,*
> *the perfect, the young one in the Aten within the arm of your mother Hathor.*

While the sun appeared as the most powerful force and the principal identity of the creator, the Egyptians did acknowledge other creative impulses. The god Ptah was considered a patron of craftsmen, perhaps originally of stoneworkers though later also of metalworkers; this creativity of the earth was shared with a falcon-headed deity Sokar, perhaps the original patron of metal crafts, and both gods of earthly creativity had their main cult centres in the area of Memphis, where the royal Residence fostered the greatest concentration of art production in the Old Kingdom. On the sarcophagus of a high priestess of Amun, Ankhnesneferibra, of the sixth century BC, one text credits Ptah with fashioning the golden clothing and image for the burial (perhaps meaning a gilt coffin and gold mask), and Sokar with the construction of the stone chamber (possibly including the great sarcophagus itself, which is all that survives of the burial). About two hundred years earlier, the Kushite king Shabako had the text from a wormeaten manuscript copied onto a slab of basalt, which survived albeit damaged from reuse as a grinding-stone. The text comprises two sections of narrative concerning deities, one relating to the contendings of Horus and Seth, and the other a remarkable text in praise of the creative power of Ptah, covering even the creation of the creator-god Atum himself.

The gods who took form as Ptah: . . . Ptah the great, being the tongue and heart of Ra . . .
The form as tongue and the form as heart are as the image of Atum; the great and mighty is Ptah who vivifies . . .
Thoth took form by it, Horus took form by it, by Ptah. It is come to pass that heart and tongue have power over [all] limbs [according to] the teaching that it is in the fore of every body, in the fore of every mouth, of all gods, all people, all herds, all snakes . . .
His Ennead is before him as the lips and teeth, the hands and semen of Atum, for the Ennead of Atum took shape through his semen and his fingers . . .
The eyes see, the ears hear, the nose breathes air; they raise to the heart, and it is then the one that makes all that has been bound together go forth, while it is the tongue that repeats what the heart has planned. That is how all gods were born, Atum and his Ennead. For, see, every word of god took form from what the heart had planned and what the tongue commanded . . .

The message of this highly intricate phrasing appears to be that creation depends on a creative impulse within a framework similar to the framework of the human body and human action; just as a human deed requires a human mind to formulate a plan, and a human tongue to pronounce it for its fulfilment, so too the emergence

25 The stela of a man named Pennub, bearing a representation of the god Ptah enthroned beneath the winged sun-disk with uraei. 19th Dynasty, c.1250 BC; limestone, from Deir el-Medina, Thebes (?). H. 23 cm. EA 8497.

of the creator and his creation required a project and a tool to enunciate the project. The role of Ptah is cast here as the creative impulse of heart and tongue, in terms strikingly close to the ancient Greek evocation of a divine mind (Greek *nous*) and the divine word at the beginning of the Gospel of Saint John (Greek *logos*). Without the impulse the creator Atum 'all matter' would never become distinguished from Nun the waters of primeval nothingness, and the world would never become differentiated as Shu and Tefnut (dry and moist), Geb and Nut (earth and sky) and so forth. In this text, although an 'image' of Atum, the heart and tongue are the preconditions for creation, reminiscent of the texts that place Heka, Hu and Sia with the creator on the eve of the birth of the world. As the god that embodies those creative principles, Ptah comes perhaps even closer to our concept of creator than Atum the Lord of the Universe.

The world of our experience can seem far removed from the most abstract investigations of creative impulses, and the ancient Egyptians did not hesitate to express the more concrete aspects of creation. Male potency took visible form in Min, a standing god with erect phallus. Min is one of the few deities whose iconography reaches back before the unification $c.3000$ BC. Damaged colossal statues of the late fourth millennium BC from his temple at Coptos show a male figure with his left hand grasped around a space in which a stone phallus would once have been, and a palette of similar date for grinding eyepaint bears the emblem later used to write the name of Min, a tubular object usually identified as a meteoritic rock. In Pharaonic art Min is shown mummiform with one arm stretched back to support a royal emblem known in Egyptology as a flail, although it was made not for punitive purposes but apparently for collecting laudanum, as still used in recent times by Eastern Mediterranean shepherds. The other distinguishing feature of Min is a tall double-plumed headdress; this was taken over by the iconography of the new god of state Amun from its inception in the early Middle Kingdom, and as a god of male fertility Amun was depicted exactly like Min and named Kamutef 'bull of his mother', that is, creator of himself. In the Middle Kingdom Min also combined with the god Horus at Abydos as 'Min-Horus-the-victorious' the potent vanquisher of Seth. As lord of the deserts Min gave protection to expeditions extracting valued materials from the mountainous and waterless wastes east of his cult centres Coptos and Akhmim. The typical representation of a sanctuary for Min recalls a desert tent, and New Kingdom temple-wall reliefs depict the ceremony of raising the tent-poles for Min; between the god and his sanctuary two-dimensional representations generally show his plant, the lettuce, considered an aphrodisiac.

Physical creativity was also perceived in the work of the potter, worshipped in the god Khnum, who was represented as a ram with curling horizontal horns,

26 The god Min (on the left) as represented on the stela of the chief royal craftsman Qeh, on which the other deities are Qedeshet, Reshep and Anat, all from Western Asia. The role of Min as master of the eastern deserts would account for his presence among these imported deities. 19th Dynasty, *c.*1250 BC; limestone, from Deir el-Medina, Thebes. H. 72 cm. EA 191.

distinct from the ram with horns curving down the side of the face, a species more recent in Egyptian art and associated with the god Amun. Although texts do not expound on the symbolism of the ram beyond its 'dignity', its importance can be seen in its use as depiction of Khnum, Amun and as evening sunlight the creator Atum; presumably, as with the bull, the ram presented a vivid instance of male potency in nature. Khnum appears in texts and images as the deity that forms human beings on the potter's wheel, as if out of clay, much as we still speak at the funeral of a person of 'ashes to ashes, dust to dust'. In the Ptolemaic and Roman Periods his principal sanctuaries were the great temples constructed at Esna and on the island of Elephantine, both in southern Upper Egypt; he could be adored as the great creator in the form Khnum-Ra first found at Elephantine in the Middle Kingdom, and the surviving hall of the temple at Esna bears hymns to the ram-god as giver of life, inscribed under the Roman emperors.

The island of Elephantine housed an earlier cult, one of the few to be traced on the ground back to the fourth millennium B C. The site began life as a hollow in the base rock, where the rise of the floodwaters would have echoed immediately before their arrival, heralding the start of the annual miracle that brought to Egypt new water with fresh silt for the fields. The deity at this shrine was not Khnum but the goddess Satet, and the relation between the two was in later times expressed in typically Egyptian style as that of husband and wife; from the New Kingdom it became the pattern to venerate in each main temple a holy family of god, goddess and divine child, on the model set by Osiris, Isis and Horus as explained in the next chapter, and in Elephantine the child of Khnum and Satet became another local goddess, Anuqet of the gazelle hunt. In this instance the relation between the god and the two goddesses never became entirely fixed, Anuqet sometimes acting more as a second consort than as a daughter to Khnum, but the pattern of a triad of deities was upheld. Although a relatively late development, the system of triads in the New Kingdom and after underlines a peculiarly important feature of Egyptian religion, the rule that groupings of deities are more important than either single deities or long stories linking a large number of deities in the manner of a classical Greek myth. Each Egyptian deity brings our attention to a particular concern of Egyptian life, whether protection or love or physical creation, but this focus is generally achieved with reference to another part of our experience; Horus cannot be the embodiment of order unless the observer also has a notion of Seth, embodiment of disorder, and Shu and Tefnut cannot embody dryness and moisture without reference both to the creator Atum and, perhaps more importantly, to one another. Like words, Egyptian gods and goddesses depend upon one another for their meaning; Shu and Tefnut complement one another as the concept of dryness depends on the complementary concept of moisture. The notion of most fundamental importance is that relations between things, rather than the things themselves, are to be expressed as divine; this is the feature that Akhenaten removed with his single godhead, the Aten, a reformation shared with the newer religions of Judaism, Christianity and Islam.

The emphasis placed on relationships may explain why the Egyptians so singularly failed to deify material features in the natural landscape, when their texts and

27 and 28 The sycamore goddess as represented on two items from burial equipment; (RIGHT) the *shabti*-box of Henutmehyt and (BELOW) the *Book of the Dead* vignette papyrus of Tameniu. In the latter both the deceased and the *ba* (soul of mobility) are shown receiving cool water from the goddess, who is in this instance identified as Nut. RIGHT 19th Dynasty, *c*.1250 BC; painted wood, from Thebes. H. 32.5 cm. EA 41549. BELOW Third Intermediate Period, *c*.950 BC; painted papyrus, from Thebes. H. (of full sheet) 28 cm. EA 10002, detail.

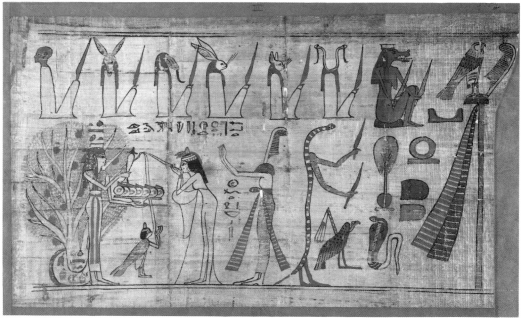

art so perfectly capture its breathtaking beauty in detail from fourth-millennium images of animals to the early Christian sermons using the lowliest forms of animal life as metaphors for the human and the divine. Animals might represent deities, as the Apis bull represented Ptah, the Buchis bull represented the Theban falcon-god Mont, or the Mnevis bull was 'herald of Ra'. In a similar vein trees might be considered sacred to a specific deity in certain instances, such as the *ished*-tree in the temple of the sun at Iunu, and the sycamore tree (in Egyptian *nehat*, a word also used for 'shelter'), which could be represented with a goddess emerging to sustain the deceased with offerings, and a mountain or field estate might be represented as a

49

29 The deity providing abundance from 'the flood',
Hapy, as depicted in this detail of the offering-table of
Imhotep. The plants on his head indicate that this is the
flood in Upper Egypt. Ptolemaic Period, third century BC
or later; limestone, from Akhmim (?). H. of full
offering-table 45 cm. EA 1688.

male or female offering-bearer yielding its produce to the ruler. Yet in all instances
the animals, birds, trees and lands appear as secondary manifestations of other
divinities; the tree-goddess may be named as Isis or as the sky-goddess Nut, but the
tree itself would not be considered a deity. When a child was named after a natural
feature, such as Sanehat, 'son of the sycamore', other texts and images make clear
that the deity envisaged was not the feature in itself, but a member of the usual
pantheon; the deity concealed in the name Sanehat would be Hathor, whose most
common epithet at Memphis was 'lady of the southern sycamore'. The moon might
be represented as a god *Iah*, 'moon', but he appears only in the Late Period and
seems in most instances to be considered a form of Osiris. Another moon-god was
Khons, perhaps, like Iah, taking over a lunar role as Thoth moved towards other
themes such as writing and knowledge; like Iah too, Khons seems to cover more
than the celestial sphere alone, and to have embodied originally the reverence for
the afterbirth of the king as an 'opener of ways' in the most literal sense. The stars
too were not worshipped in themselves but for their relation to other beings; the
circumpolar stars that never set in the night sky comprised one channel of hope for
resurrection in the *Pyramid Texts*, where the deceased is directed to become an
'imperishable star' and so live forever; the star Sirius was deified as a goddess Sepdet
for its role in heralding the first days of the inundation every summer.

This attitude to the natural environment extended even to the river Nile itself,
which was simply termed *iteru*, 'the river', in later times *na i(te)ru*, 'the river-bran-
ches', from which the Greek word Neilos and our word Nile seem to be derived.
The life-giving force of the silt-rich floodwaters were acknowledged as a deity
Hapy, 'the flood', but of a peculiar character. Hapy appears in two- and three-
dimensional art as a man with pendulous breasts and bearing the plentiful produce
of the earth after the inundation; he received worship not through a regular cult
with temple and priesthood but through great annual offerings. The annual
offering to the flood may have provided if not the actual setting then the inspiration
for a great literary work, probably of the Middle Kingdom but known only from
New Kingdom copies, the *Hymn to the Flood*. In it, the humble mud and water of
the flood are recognised as more critical to life than fabulous treasures:

there is no-one whose hand weaves with gold,
there is nobody who becomes drunk with silver,
true lapis lazuli cannot be eaten;
barley is the fundament of well-being . . .
when you rise for the hungering town-dwellers,
they sate themselves on the produce of the country . . .
goodness is strewn in the streets,
and the whole land frolics afoot.

The picture of the floodwaters recalls the less positive imagery of the primeval waters of nothingness, out of which matter emerged but in which the world hangs in delicate balance. The potential for creation in the primeval waters afforded the hope for renewal just as the sun was regenerated daily in the night hours for its dawn birth. The potency of the night or of the dark waters of pre-existence was expressed not only as Nun the seas of nothingness, but also as a more motherly figure in the classic Egyptian metaphor for motherly care, the cow caring for its calf. The cow of primeval waters was named Mehytweret, 'the great inundation', a deity present above all in funerary literature from the *Pyramid Texts* on; another name for the same phenomenon was Ihet, also represented as a cow and sometimes expressly identified as Mehytweret. Still another expression of the waters out of which land emerged was Neit, a goddess whose main temple stood at Sais and whose role included the masculine territory of hunt and warfare; Neit as aggressive water formed the natural mother, in Egyptian expression, to the crocodile Sobek, a god revered particularly at dangerous riverbanks where the threat of crocodiles loomed especially large, as at Rizeiqat and Kom Ombo in Upper Egypt, as well as more generally throughout the marshes of the Fayum. The cultivation of the Fayum in the Middle Kingdom promoted Sobek to the rank of dynastic patron, and his combination with universal power was expressed in the usual formula with the sun-god as Sobek-Ra.

Sobek-Ra returns us with an air of inevitability to the supreme role of the sun. A more complex and evocative example of the same principle is the deity at Djedet (Mendes in Greek) in the Delta. The god of Mendes was a ram named simply Banebdjed, 'the spirit, the lord of Djedet', incorporating the creative essence of the world in four forms or '*ba*-spirits', which corresponded to the four first rulers of the world, Ra, Shu, Geb and Osiris. In the sixth century BC the Saite king of Egypt Ahmose II had constructed at Mendes four vast monolithic granite shrines, one for each 'spirit', transforming the site into one of the most impressive monumental complexes in Egypt until its destruction, perhaps from natural causes, toward the end of Ptolemaic rule. The quadruple shrine of Mendes cast in stone the Egyptian theory of order, that kingship passes from one emanation of the sun to another, to preserve creation and maintain the triumph of Right over Wrong. That struggle, seen in the revolt against Ra, found its most compelling mirror in the cycle of myths of Osiris and Horus.

2

POWER ON EARTH

Osiris and Horus

LIKE AMUN, OSIRIS DOES NOT APPEAR in the record until the funerary texts for king Unas were recorded on the inner chambers of his pyramid $c.$ 2400 BC, but the deity went on from that point to assume a leading role in Egyptian religious texts and images. It may be more than coincidence that the same period, the Pyramid Age, saw the development of mummification; the Egyptians depicted Osiris as a mummiform man with a crown called *atef* and comprising an ostrich-feather either side of the tall White Crown worn by the king. Osiris was strictly speaking the god not of the dead in general but of the blessed dead, the dead who had led good lives. Indeed, in the surviving record of texts and images formulated for the wealthier sectors of society, the blessed dead are defined still more narrowly as those who had received a good burial including the costly procedure of being mummified. Since mummification involved immersion in a tub of dry natron, wrapping in fine (if never new) linen strips, and dousing with unguents and resins, it was, even at the cheapest end of the market, an expensive business, and can never have been available to the very poor. In the formal record Osiris remained as he began his existence, the god of the dead king and his court, of the upper strata of society. The texts recognise the palpable injustice of this scheme by emphasising that the good not the rich survive death, a moral that finds its literary climax in the tale of Setne-Khaemwaset and his son Sawesir, a composition of the Ptolemaic or Roman Period. Setne and his son see a rich and a poor funeral on earth and later, on a visit to the underworld, they witness the tortures of the same rich man and the blessed afterlife of the same poor man.

The cult centre of Osiris in Upper Egypt was at Abydos, where the first kings of Egypt were buried and where a temple to Khentamentiu, 'foremost of the Wester-ners (i.e. the dead)', existed already in the Old Kingdom. Khentamentiu may have

30 Tomb-chapel door of Khonshotep, high priest of Amun, with a scene depicting Osiris enthroned in the company of Hathor, mistress of the western desert, receiving the adoration of Khonshotep. Early 19th Dynasty, $c.$ 1285 BC (?); wood, from Thebes. H. 2.4 m. EA 705.

been the embodiment of all dead kings, and his cult was absorbed by Osiris toward the end of the Old Kingdom; in one sense Osiris is a new form of the old god, Khentamentiu seen through the prism of mummification. Mummification aimed to preserve the body, but, as is seen in chapter five, this end could be achieved only by violating the integrity of the body in order to remove softer and more rapidly decaying organs; thus it involved violence just as death itself involves violence, and it could not take place without the violent and disorderly force of Seth. The first level of the Osiris and Horus cycle begins therefore with an act of violence by Seth against Osiris.

The image of the god Seth forms one of the most brilliant achievements of a goal in Egyptian art. Faced with the task of presenting the essence of disorder in a clear manner that does not disrupt the general harmony of the surrounding composition, the artists put together a series of bodily features that do not quite occur in the natural environment of Egypt, assembling a neat photo-fit portrayal of disorderliness. Seth thus acquired a tail with a forked end, a curving snout and two tall straight-topped ears. This creature first appeared among the first texts at the founding of the Egyptian state $c.$ 3000 BC, as counterpart to the falcon Horus, but the first texts to expound on his nature are the veiled references in the *Pyramid Texts*, where already he stands as the enemy and murderer of his brother Osiris. Egyptian texts tend to be reticent on the catastrophic moment of murder, but the ritual for the 'end of (mummification) operations' gives a brusque summary, from the moment that Osiris first arrived at Abydos:

Osiris then said 'how great is this land', which is called Tawer ('great land' = the province of Abydos) to this day; then Osiris was perfect within it exceedingly greatly; then Seth heard him; Seth came in haste, and arrived against Osiris within Nedyt in Hatdjefau (two places in the area of Abydos) under a tree called aru *in the first month of inundation, day 17, and committed an act of great violence against him, and had him sunk in the waters; then Nun rose to cover him exceedingly greatly, and he was borne away to hide his mysteries ...*

The text goes on to describe the cosmos in chaos at the death of Osiris, and the tears of the gods turning into materials used in mummification such as honey, resins and incense; the rest of the ritual prescribes the fashioning of statues of enemies, to be destroyed, and of Osiris, to be mummified and buried.

The date in the ritual does not agree with the usual date given for the death of Osiris, presumably because the ritual tailored the myth to suit the time of year that it was due to be performed; the place of the murder, under an *aru*-tree in the area of Abydos, is more in keeping with other texts. In the Middle Kingdom the tomb of king Djer, one of the first kings of Egypt, was reinterpreted as the tomb of Osiris and became the goal of annual processions in which the murder of Osiris and his vindication by Horus were re-enacted; a sculptural effigy of the body of Osiris on the funerary bier was installed in the tomb of Djer by a late Middle Kingdom king, probably Khendjer, although the name has been erased.

From the late Old Kingdom officials passing Abydos on commission from the northern Residence to Upper Egypt not only stopped to participate in the festivals but also to have offering-chapels for their own funerary cult constructed as near as

31 The god Seth as depicted on the stela of the royal craftsman Aapehty. For the harmony of the composition the artist has balanced the figure of the god against that of the human worshipper by combining human body with composite animal head. 19th Dynasty, *c.* 1250 BC; limestone, from Deir el-Medina, Thebes. H. 21.2 cm. EA 35630.

32 The stela from an Abydos offering-chapel for a man called Amunerhatef, shown in the lower register in adoration of Osiris who is seated above at a table of offerings. 19th Dynasty, *c*.1250 BC; limestone, from Abydos. H. 28 cm. EA 345.

possible to the route taken by festival processions from the temple of Osiris to his tomb. Certain kings shared in this movement to be near to Osiris at Abydos in concrete funerary form, and so constructed cenotaphs in which they cemented their identity with the dead king Osiris for the perpetuity of their own funerary cults. Senusret III in the late Middle Kingdom and Ahmose I in the early New Kingdom each set up large-scale monuments at the southern reaches of the cemeteries there, but the most impressive surviving monuments are the temples constructed by Sety I and his son Ramses II, the former with an additional grave of Osiris sunk low in the sand behind his temple, with water around a central island to which a sloping corridor descends as if to the underworld itself. In funerary texts the deceased is said to visit Abydos and Busiris, the Lower Egyptian cult centre of Osiris, and these journeys are often termed the 'Osirian pilgrimages'. The term is a misnomer, however, because there is no evidence that any Egyptian ever set out on a voyage with the sole aim of participating in rites at another place, in the way that Christians go to Jerusalem or Moslems make the journey to Mecca. Rather the funerary texts set out to establish the identity of the deceased with the divinity that will help to secure a good afterlife, and in the case of Osiris this involves partaking of visits to Busiris and Abydos on a spiritual plane. The same principle gave rise to a series of funerary texts in the Middle and New Kingdoms for knowing the *ba*-spirits of the ancient cities Buto and Nekhen (Hieraconpolis) as well as Abydos and the city of Thoth Khemenu (Hermopolis). Other funerary texts seek to provide access to the Memphite necropolis Rosetjau (modern Giza), to reserve for the deceased a seat in Iunu (Heliopolis) and to avoid slaughter in Hennesut (Heracleopolis). In all instances the placenames transfer important features of the religious landscape of Egypt to a symbolic level, and reveal the national prestige of those places without implying national pilgrimages to any of them.

The murder of Osiris by Seth required that Osiris be brought back to life by his sister and wife Isis, and so in a sense the murderous Seth was needed for the cycle of regeneration and rebirth. Similar treatment occurs in the process of mummification: one man was required to cut open the flank of the body for the retrieval of the softer inner organs; he was then, according to ancient Greek accounts, forced to flee the embalming tent pursued by his stone-throwing colleagues. Seth likewise came to be demonised as absolute evil in later periods of Egyptian history, his name and image erased. The murder of Osiris set a model copied in the process of mummification, but the promise of new life, awakened by the power of Isis, was also seen in the natural cycle of seeds sown in the fresh silt left by the annual flood to become the rich harvest for which Egypt was famed in Biblical and classical Greek and Roman antiquity. The equation of Osiris with the miracle of harvest occurs particularly vividly in a text inscribed on the sarcophagus of Ankhnesneferibra, where the gods mourn the murdered Osiris:

> Hail, you are Osiris the great on the riverbanks, at whose wish Hapy emerges from his cavern.
> Hail, you are Osiris the falcon on earth, the falcon of electrum within the sky.
> Hail, you are the maker of grain, he who gives life to the gods with the water of his limbs, and bread to every land with the water that takes form under him.

The text then explains, 'barley has taken form out of the limbs of Osiris, when Thoth placed him in the Good Domain (= embalming workshop)', and Thoth is said to observe, 'the plants that took form with you are the grain which he made to create mankind'. The role of Osiris as fertility as well as funerary god provoked the opposition of Akhenaten in his refinement of Egyptian cult to the one focus of the sun-disk; Osiris is absent at Akhetaten and the agents of the king destroyed the images of that other incarnation of the fertility of the flood, Hapy. Akhenaten took for himself the role of fertility god, most dramatically in the colossal statues of himself with female features in the temple to the sun constructed by him to the east of the Amun temple at Karnak. When the gods were restored in the reign of Tutankhamun, the separate concern for fertility received particular attention in statues such as those of Hapy and of Amun in the form of Min.

In the second century A D the Greek writer Plutarch compiled a connected narrative concerning Osiris, in which episodes of the cycle are recounted in chronological order, but it is difficult to assess how many episodes reflect later development of the story, or how much the sequence is influenced by the conventions of classical Greek myth. For example, Plutarch recounts how Seth tricked his brother Osiris into lying in a cedarwood coffin at a banquet, after promising it to the man whom it fitted the most tightly. This episode may have been developed at a late stage, perhaps even by or for the benefit of a Greek audience, as a more concrete rendering of the parallel between the murder and the procedure of mummification and burial in a fine coffin. Similarly the version in Plutarch has two murders of Osiris by Seth with two acts of revivification by the power of Isis; this may be a late, again perhaps Greek, device to harmonise different versions of the murder. Later Greek commentators, in their ignorance of the Egyptian language, were perhaps over-literal in their understanding of the myth; the Egyptians were more open in their expression of the unknowable, accepting different detailed versions as the human renderings of divine and so inexpressible relations.

The core message of the first part of the cycle is that Osiris was murdered by Seth, and that Isis brought him back to life. The only other feature that remains constant is that Seth not only slew his brother but dismembered the body, a further crime that underlines both the horror of the act and the extraordinary power of Isis to be able to bring her husband-brother back to life. In late tradition each part of Egypt was home to one relic of the god; Plutarch recounts that the phallus alone was lost, swallowed by an oxyrhynchus-fish, but Egyptian pictorial and textual sources refute this detail, apparently borrowed from an incident in classical Greek mythology. Isis now demonstrated her power by not only reassembling Osiris and bringing him back to life but even conceiving a son by him. After the conception,

33 Hapy, the deity bringing the abundance of the flood, shown here with the distinctive features of Tutankhamun. This is one of the considerable number of statues of deities set up in the restoration of the cults of the gods after the interruption in the reign of Akhenaten. After the death of Tutankhamun the statue was inscribed with the name of Horemheb. 18th Dynasty, c. 1325 BC; black granite, of unknown provenance. H. (including restored base) 1.68 m. EA 75.

dramatically portrayed in concealed temple reliefs, Osiris withdrew to rule the underworld, while Isis took her son to the marshes. Here the second stage in the drama begins, with the birth of the infant Horus and the efforts of his mother to defend him from the forces of evil; the defenceless child rested in the Delta marshes, like Moses in the bullrushes, and only the power of Isis could ward off or cure the bites of wild animals that in some cases still curse the life of the Egyptian in the countryside – scorpions, poisonous snakes, crocodiles.

This part of the cycle created a framework for endless recourse to Isis in the difficulties of the real world; attempts to cope with venomous bites and the danger of crocodiles were supported by appeals to Isis and, from texts on papyrus at least as early as $c.$ 1750 BC, full identifications of the patient with the infant Horus. The mythic prototype also offered a model of hope for mothers with child, when identity of mother and child directly as Isis and Horus promised an escape from the danger of death at the most vulnerable stage in the life cycle. Once the frame had been established, it was possible to develop an infinite number of variants on the same theme in the effort to escape the suffering caused by animal bites. One of the most literary extensions of the genre is the tale of Isis and the seven scorpions, in which a noblewoman closes her door to Isis, who is then given shelter by a poor fisher-girl; the seven scorpions avenge Isis by combining their venom in one sting and inflicting it on the son of the rich woman. Isis takes pity on the child and cures him, whereupon the contrite noblewoman rewards the poor fisher girl. This episode survives with the image of Horus on a papyrus and on stelae, objects that were used in the practical fight against disease. However, its openly moralistic tone strongly indicates that it was devised as a new composition in a literary framework and did not derive from a more ancient stock of myth. As with the murder of Osiris, certain features of the childhood of Horus remain constant across a wide body of texts, images and periods. Isis flees Seth at the advice of Thoth, and gives birth to the infant Horus in the remote Delta marshes of Akhbit (rendered Chemmis in Greek) described by Greek authors as a floating island; Isis protects the child during his infancy against all dangers, above all against the two most common dangers in the country, scorpions and serpents, until as an adolescent he can stand against Seth to claim his rightful inheritance, the throne of Egypt.

With the fight of Horus against Seth for the throne of his father Osiris the cycle moves into its third and final phase. The pairing of Horus and Seth is the oldest feature of the cycle, antedating the first attestations of Osiris by six centuries or more. Texts and images of unification set the falcon Horus in pre-eminent place as the title of kingship and personification of divine and regal power. The Egyptian king first appears in the textual record as the god Horus in his form in the palace, an earthly manifestation of celestial power, before even Ra the sun-god played any part in the recorded activity of kingship. At the same time a Seth-figure appears in

34 A figure of Isis wearing cowhorns and a solar disk and preparing to suckle the child Horus on her lap. Late Period, after 600 BC; bronze, of unknown provenance. H. 28 cm. EA 11131.

35 Stone vessel for ointment inscribed with the Horus-name and throne-name cartouche of Djedkara Isesi between the protecting goddesses Wadjyt, the cobra of Lower Egypt, and Nekhbet, the vulture of Upper Egypt, each extending to the royal names the *shen* or ring of sovereignty. 5th Dynasty, *c*. 2400 BC; calcite, of unknown provenance. H. 7.6 cm. EA 57322.

royal inscriptions with the phonetic hieroglyphs Ash or Sha. The latter recurs in Middle Kingdom depictions as the label to a Seth-animal in the desert, and the word is perhaps the same as *sha*, 'countryside', in the sense of the disorderly fringe of the country where fertile Nile Valley meets waterless Saharan deserts. In the Second Dynasty the Seth-animal appears in place of the falcon in the writing of one royal name, conventionally read Peribsen although a fuller writing suggests the long form Peribienmaat, 'my heart goes forth to Right', with abbreviated form Perenesibi, 'my heart goes forth to her'. The same king moved the royal burial place back from Saqqara, probable site of the early Second Dynasty burials, to the First Dynasty royal necropolis Umm el-Gaab at Abydos. In what may have been the next reign the Horus falcon and Seth-animal meet directly for the first time, facing one another atop the palace frame enclosing a new and programmatic royal name Khasekhemwy, 'the two powers are risen'. Khasekhemwy also had his tomb built at Abydos alongside that of Peribsen, but at the cult centre of Horus at Hieraconpolis he left monuments in the shorter name Khasekhem, 'the power is risen', topped only by the falcon, and his statues – the earliest surviving royal stone sculpture from Egypt – have around their bases the contorted figures of slain enemies. The political implications and even the exact sequence of these name changes remain obscure; the Seth-animal was erased from the tombstone of Peribsen, but this may have occurred at a later date. The next kings moved their necropolis back to Saqqara, and the precarious balance of Horus falcon and Seth-animal came gradually to fall under the shadow of the single emphasis on Ra. This early history of the balance or imbalance between Horus and Seth is all but lost in the shadows of the record.

The confrontation of the two deities Horus and Seth is clearer when they stand

36 Free-standing stela from the superstructure of the tomb of king Peribsen, with the figure of the Seth animal erased over the rectangle containing the name of the king. 2nd Dynasty, c.2800 BC; granite, from Abydos. H. 1.13 m. EÁ 35597.

not on their own but in the legacy of Osiris, in the late Old Kingdom and afterwards. When set against the background of the murder of Osiris, Seth is more clearly the wrongdoer and Horus the champion of order. Like the tribulations of Isis in the marshes with her infant, the battle between the forces of order, Horus, and those of disorder, Seth, could be elaborated endlessly, for example, in the Ramesside literary tale of the contendings of Horus and Seth, and in a great series of reliefs on walls of the temple of Horus at Edfu dating to the Ptolemaic Period. The core message of this part of the story lies in the effort needed to achieve the final victory of Horus over Seth; it should also be noted that until the first millennium B C Seth was not considered to have been cast entirely out of the world of order, but became incorporated into it as the disruptive force needed alongside perfect order to keep the world in motion. The Egyptian sources agree upon a number of details in the conflict, including physical duels on land and water. In these battles the two gods exert their *hem*, a word usually translated 'majesty' and most commonly used with reference to the king as conventionally rendered 'your majesty'. The word seems to encapsulate more the notion of any physical agency that can achieve the designs of a person, and for that reason is used even of the bulk of the serving population in the Middle Kingdom as *hem-nesut*, 'servant (correctly 'physical agent') of the king'.

The clash of the physical forces unleashed by the two gods sees them transforming themselves into animals such as the hippopotamus, but also takes more subtle form, in the attempts of each deity to win his case by argument. Indeed the final decision has to be taken by the tribunal of the gods, like a legal decision over inheritance. Isis plays an ambivalent role, being drawn to Seth as her brother but more strongly and decisively to Horus as her son; at one point her wavering provokes the wrath of Horus who is said, in the literary Ramesside version, to behead his mother and is punished for this by losing his eyes. This is a variant of the principal damage inflicted by each god on the other, Horus taking the testicles of Seth and Seth taking the eye of Horus, as already cited in the *Pyramid Texts*. The testicles of Seth express his sexual potency, a prime source of his disruptive powers, while the eye of Horus expresses his clarity of vision and omniscience, much as the eye of Ra is a metaphor for the power of the creator. In each case the loss of a part of the body becomes a way of defining the essential character and power of the god; the eye of Horus, like the eye of Ra, has to be restored, and every offering in cult could be presented as the same deed of restoring the eye to the god, a theme developed to most elaborate extent in the offering lists of the *Pyramid Texts*. The sexual drive of Seth is embodied in another episode, attested both in the Ramesside tale and in a late Middle Kingdom literary precursor, in which Seth rapes Horus and thereby proves his superiority; the reversal of fortune can only be rectified when Isis tricks Seth into eating his own semen, placed on his favourite food, the aphrodisiac lettuce, so that when Seth calls forth his semen in the presence of the divine tribunal, it appears not on Horus but on himself, making a mockery of his claim to the inheritance of Osiris.

In the Ramesside tale of the contendings this episode is followed by a further duel, a ship race, in which Seth's ship sinks; he then turns himself again into a hippopotamus, whereupon Horus strikes him with a harpoon. The scene of the hippopotamus-hunt in tomb-chapels places the tomb-owner in the role of Horus defending order against anarchy in a specific mythic episode.

After the contendings come the judgments, and the sources agree that there were two stages in concluding the struggle. In the first settlement, Horus was given one half of the dominion of Osiris on earth, and Seth received the other half; different sources give different accounts of exactly what comprises half of the Two Lands, the name given to Pharaonic Egypt in the title of the king as 'lord of the Two Lands'. Sometimes the halves are Upper and Lower Egypt, sometimes the cultivated valley and the uninhabitable desert, but the principle of a division of the kingship of Osiris remains the same. This arrangement was then considered un-workable and Horus was given the undivided kingship, as heir of Osiris and, through him, Geb, Shu and ultimately Ra himself. Seth did not disappear from the ordered world, but became the defender of Ra by standing at the prow of the solar bark and channelling his anarchic energy to fight off the more sinister forces of annihilation that threatened to engulf the sun on its journey through the day and night sky. Thunder was said to be the voice of Seth, and in hieroglyphs the word for 'storm', *neshen*, is given a Seth-animal as its determinative or ending-sign. Each king incorporated both Seth and Horus, as depicted on the sides of thrones for some statues where Horus and Seth tie together the plants of Upper and Lower Egypt to create the hieroglyph for 'union'. Yet the god Horus was always the foremost god of kingship, and each royal accession was acclaimed as the vindi-cation of Horus over the enemies of order, the rise of the son of the sun-god to replace the darkness of disorder or pre-existence with the light of order and the sun. A Ramesside hymn greets the accession of Merenptah, son and successor of Ramses II, as the triumph of good over evil:

> *Let your hearts be glad, entire land, good times are come.*
> *The lord, given life, prosperity, health, is risen over all lands.*
> *Order is gone down to its place.*
> *Dual king, lord of millions of years,*
> *great in kingship in the likeness of Horus,*
> *Baenra-beloved-of-Amun, who drives Egypt with festivals,*
> *son of Ra, most luminary of all kings,*
> *Merenptah-content-upon-Right, given life, prosperity, health.*
> *All you people of Right, come and see:*
> *Right drives off Falsehood,*
> *the people of Wrong are cast on their faces,*
> *all the rapacious are rejected.*
> *The water is standing, does not subside, the flood bears aloft;*
> *the days are long, the nights have hours,*
> *the moon is come correctly.*
> *The gods are satisfied and contented,*
> *and we live in laughing and wonders.*

The accession of the king marks the same triumph as that of the sun-god emerging out of nothingness, but also as that of Horus coming to the throne as king at the end of his struggles with Seth. Upon this accession depend the well-being of deities and of humanity and the perfection of the natural order, above all the flood and the ordained division of day and night time. The triumph of each new Horus, each king, merges with the message of sunrise to unite the natural with the social order, the human with the divine; Horus was accordingly the first identity of the king, who took at accession a Horus-name, depicted in two-dimensional form as the *ka* or sustaining spirit of the sovereign.

The justification of Horus before the tribunal of the gods gave meaning and form also to the world beyond the grave. In the Middle Kingdom the tribunal of the afterlife is cited in the *Coffin Texts* only as a regular Egyptian court where petition could be made concerning any affair that one wished to settle in the public domain, anything that we might call a legal case. In the transition from the Middle to the New Kingdom the tribunal suddenly became not an arbitration board within the next life but a passport control point for permission to enter that life at all. The deceased was led by Horus to his father Osiris and a tribunal of forty-two assessor deities who witnessed the weighing of his heart against the figure of Right. If the

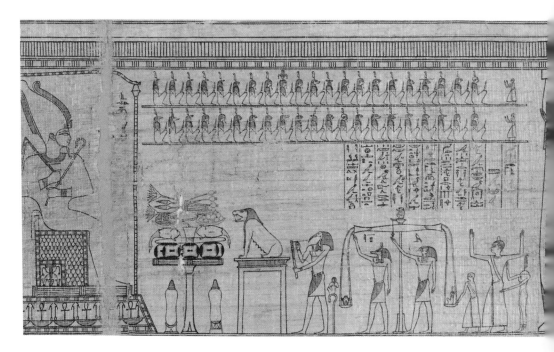

37 The judgment scene in a *Book of the Dead* in which the space for the name is left blank; on other sheets of the same papyrus the space has been filled in for the man who bought it, Ankhwahibra. The deceased raises his hands in triumph as his heart is weighed against a figure of Right (Maat); Anubis and Horus operate the scales while Thoth records the result next to the monster Amemet, who would swallow the souls of the damned. Osiris presides over the tribunal, represented as forty-two deities in two rows above the weighing scene. Late Period, 4th century BC or later; papyrus, of unknown provenance. H. 26 cm. EA 10558, part.

heart did not prove full of goodness but was instead shown to be wracked with wrongs committed against society and against the divine order, then the person could not enter the underworld, the kingdom of Osiris. If the deceased passed the test, he or she would be declared to be like Horus, 'true-of-voice', that is 'justified' in the eyes of the tribunal; this tag of 'justification' permitted entry into the company of the blessed dead. The deceased thus acquired both an identity as Osiris, guaranteeing resurrection with Osiris in his Underworld, and the quality of Horus, as 'true-of-voice', and from the New Kingdom to the Roman Period those two designations almost invariably occur respectively before and after the name of the person in funerary contexts.

In all three stages the Osiris cycle yielded guarantees for the Egyptians: the first stage, the murder and revivification of Osiris, promised fresh life in the ground, fresh plant life after the flood and fresh human existence after death; the second stage, the protection of the infant Horus, offered survival in the face of natural attack from venomous neighbours in the Nile Valley; the third stage, the struggle of Horus for victory over Seth, offered the model for kingship, for all good in the fight against evil, and for eternal life, available only to those who could prove that they had lived good lives on earth. The wide reach of the cycle explains its longevity and, perhaps, its appeal outside Egypt in the classical Greek and Roman world. Part of that appeal lay in the figure that most fully ties these three otherwise self-sufficient sets of stories together, the goddess Isis. Although Horus appears at the end of the first stage of the cycle, and Osiris is implicit in the second and third, and though Seth lurks in the background as the menace to mother and child in the second stage, only Isis performs an active role to the fore in all three.

Isis first appears, like Osiris and their sister Nephthys, in the *Pyramid Texts* inscribed for king Unas $c.2400$ BC. Although her name is written with the hieroglyph for a throne and she is generally represented as a woman wearing this emblem on her head, it is debatable whether she was considered by the Egyptians as the personification of the throne because no hymn to Isis ever presents this as part of her nature. The Egyptologist Jürgen Osing has suggested that the name derives from the word *was*, 'to have power', giving an original form Aset, 'she who has power'. Whether or not this is the true etymology, it strikes the very core of her role in texts and images, as the goddess who excels in the display of power to overcome obstacles, particularly those found in the animal world. Isis reverses the bestial act of Seth, his fratricidal attack on Osiris, and she wards off or cures the bites of poisonous creatures; she complements the creative power with a defensive power that does not wreak havoc like the fury of Sekhmet but operates surgically to remove each threat to life and health. Isis might be called the healer in human existence; she is the doctor sent by Ra to deliver his sons in the literary tale of the divine birth of kings, and her knowledge is technical and precise like that of the medical scientist. Perhaps the very precision of her actions explains why she should have become such a common resort for medical help while never receiving her own temple. In the Old Kingdom she shared to a small degree in the cult centre of Hathor at Qusae in Middle Egypt, and during the Middle and New Kingdoms her cult and priesthood became established alongside that of Osiris at Abydos and Min at Coptos among others, but her role was secondary. It is particularly astonishing that her profile was not higher at Abydos itself.

In the fourth century BC the last native Pharaohs of all Egypt overturned this curious lack of shrines to Isis and founded two magnificent new precincts in which the goddess would rule alone, one at Philae in Upper Egypt and one near their dynastic hometown Sebennytos at Behbeit in Lower Egypt. The shrine at Behbeit would have been perhaps the most impressive monument, but the majority of visitors to Egypt are familiar rather with the temple of Isis on the island of Philae, at

38 Details from the coffin of a woman named Tentmutengebtiu. It depicts, at the top, Osiris in the form of a *djed*-pillar wearing a plumed sun-disk and with arms to hold the crook and flail; he is between Isis and Nephthys who both carry the *ankh* symbol of life on their arms. In the lower register the gods Horus and Thoth purify the deceased with water represented by two streams of *ankh* and *was* symbols, the hieroglyphs for life and power. Third Intermediate Period, *c*.900 BC; painted cartonnage, from Thebes. EA 22939, part.

the door to Nubia on the southern threshold of Egypt. The Ptolemies were generous patrons to the temple, and it grew on its perfect setting until its structures covered most of the island, named by nineteenth-century visitors the Jewel of the Nile. While the rest of Egypt had first adopted a Mediterranean lifestyle under Roman rule and then converted to Christianity, the nomadic peoples in the southeastern deserts still celebrated the festivals of the goddess, and the shrine was among the few to be still functioning when the Byzantine emperor Justinian ordered the closure of the last temples in the sixth century AD.

The belief in the power of Isis and Osiris to protect, particularly to preserve the dead body from harm and decay, can be seen in the amulets associated with them in later periods, the *tit*-knot and the *djed*-pillar. Both forms occur well before the first mention of either deity and were presumably adopted as symbols of their efficacy in the world. The *tit*-knot may originally have been a knot of cloth indistinguishable from early forms of the *ankh* sign for 'life'; when the two were differentiated, the *tit* had side-ends hanging downward and clear doubling of the strip of cloth, while the *ankh* tended to be of a single less clearly divided or folded strip and its side-ends project straight out at right angles to the central strip and loop. By the early New Kingdom *c.* 1500 BC the *tit* had become the subject of a funerary text in the corpus which we call the *Book of the Dead*, with an incantation opening 'incantation for the *tit* of red jasper: you have your blood, Isis' and specifying 'for whomsoever this is recited, the defensive power of Isis will be the protection of his body, and Horus son of Isis will rejoice over him when he sees him'. The *djed*-pillar appears more stylised even in its earliest attestations and for this reason has eluded any one convincing interpretation, although it may have represented a tree-trunk and branches. The word *djed* means 'stability' or 'solidity', and the pillar embodied the solidity of the tree-trunk or, using a human analogy, the back-bone. The latter image is the one used in the parallel incantation from the *Book of the Dead*, which starts: 'Incantation for the *djed* of gold: stand, Osiris, you have your back, O weary-hearted, you have your ribs, O weary-hearted'. The adoption of both motifs gives an indication not only of the breadth of appeal of the deities in the Osiris cycle but just as importantly their faculty for accumulating existing symbolism from other sources. This fluidity in the history of Egyptian deities may be explicable in part by the sheer length of their historical lives, spanning up to three thousand years in the record of Pharaonic art and texts, but it testifies also to the poetic nature of those images. If the *djed* can become back-bone or tree, if it can refer to creator, Osiris, or king, this can only take place because all of these are as words in the hands of a poet; they are open within the grammatical rules of Egyptian religion to different formulations of a same central truth, in this instance that good endures and, implicitly, that it needs and finds protection.

3

PRESERVING THE UNIVERSE

Kingship and Cult

THE EGYPTIANS CONCEIVED OF THE WORLD, as seen in chapter one, as a solar process from sunset through sunrise to sunset endlessly repeated, a harmony that had been disturbed by the murder of Osiris by Seth. The damage to creation could be contained so long as the sun-god was represented on earth by a king who caused Right to exist, and so long as Right was raised up to her lord the sun-god by the gods Thoth or Inheret, 'he who brings back the distant goddess', by their earthly counterpart the king and by his substitutes in the different localities of Egypt, the priests. Only this framework of Right caused to exist and raised to the creator could provide the space in which human beings might in their turn participate in the task of preserving the cosmos by saying and doing Right. The conception of the universe as a fragile entity that was perpetually threatened with oblivion gave to the Egyptian cult of the gods an urgency and an extension beyond the bounds of what the Christian and Islamic traditions hold proper to worship. The most important differences are, first, the localisation of deities as separate entities in each separate place and, second, the offerings of not only words but also material food, drink and clothing. The closest analogy to the Egyptian temple thus becomes not the church or mosque in which the faithful congregate to offer prayers and hymns but the power station in which society produces the energy it needs to function and survive. An Egyptian temple is a machine for the preservation of the universe, a technical operation that requires technical staff and knowledge and thereby excludes the great majority of the population in order to ensure that the crucial task of survival is never impaired.

The maintenance of order in the face of chaos reached every part of the land, the difference between localities being expressed in the difference between the deities. The notion of 'gods of provinces' and 'gods of towns' formed a crucial binding medium in Egyptian society, specified in the Bersha funerary text cited in chapter

39 Representations of king Sety I embraced by the gods Thoth (left) and Horus (right) on the pillars in his rock-cut tomb in the Valley of the Kings at Thebes. Watercolours by Henry Salt.

40 Figure of Mont-Ra, wearing the sun-disk and double plumes and the royal kilt; each hand once held a sceptre. The double uraues in front of the sun-disk is characteristic of the deity Mont and has not been satisfactorily explained; it may express power over the Two Lands or, since it is not generally worn by kings or other gods, is perhaps a device to distinguish him from the other falcon-headed gods of power. Late Period, after 600 BC; bronze with gilt silver necklace, of unknown provenance. H. 20 cm. EA 60342.

one as one of the four good deeds of the creator: 'I made their hearts not forget the West, from the wish that divine offerings be made to the local deities'. Some of these 'local' deities, such as Ptah of Memphis and Amun of Thebes, had national importance, that is they received worship in shrines throughout the country, but their role as local deity was made explicit in epithets such as 'lord of such-and-such a province/town' or in specific forms such as Horus-of-Nekhen who appeared as a mummiform falcon on a shrine in contrast to the usual representations of Horus as a falcon or falcon-headed man. Other deities are known only from one area or locality, such as Mont, the falcon deity whose cult centres lay at four towns in the Theban province, Armant, Tod, Medamud and Thebes itself. In the New Kingdom Mont appears more widely as the deity equipping the king with the weapons

72

for his victories, but his tendencies to universalism were expressed in the usual way as a compound with the sun-god Mont-Ra. Other local deities include the felines Pakhet, 'the scratcher', who took the role of raging leonine goddess at the limestone quarries in the desert valley south-east of Beni Hasan in Middle Egypt, and Maihesa, 'the wild lion', worshipped as son of the leonine goddesses Bast and Sekhmet in the Delta cities Bubastis and Taremu (rendered Leontopolis, 'city of the lion', by the Greeks). Another Delta deity was Hatmehyt, 'the first of the inundation', represented as a fish and worshipped at Mendes. Some deities are restricted in the record not only to certain places but more strikingly to specific times, such as the goddess of the Theban necropolis Merseger, 'lover of silence', known above all from texts and monuments left by the craftsmen of the royal tomb in the New Kingdom.

It is sometimes suggested that the local deities reflect a prehistoric stage of religion in which different communities each had their own deity in the form of a standard or symbol, a stage denoted fetishism by historians of religion. The different local traditions would then, according to this theory, join together to form the full pantheon in the process of political unification that culminated in the emergence of the single state $c.3000\,BC$. This theory seems to be a projection of modern notions of progress onto a conveniently blank record of prehistoric religious practice in Egypt, confined to only a few objects and representations and, self-evidently, no texts. When the record first unfolds in the early centuries of the Egyptian state $c.3000-2500\,BC$ it yields a single pantheon without features that could logically be split into different religions. The early attestations for Horus, Seth, Ptah, Min and Khnum do not speak for separate groups of belief in each deity, because each deity occupies a different space in human experience so that, for example, Ptah denotes a different type of creativity to Khnum or Min. Most decisively, each god delineates an area of experience only by reference to other deities, most obviously in the complementary pairing of Horus and Seth, but equally in the binary union of Nekhbet and Wadjyt. These pairs are not speculation on the part of a modern observer; they occur concretely as motifs on ancient objects. It is better therefore to regard the pantheon as a means of perceiving divinity that already existed in the fourth millennium BC, a unified system of beliefs corresponding to the homogeneous culture of Nile Valley farmers spreading from Upper Egypt $c.4000\,BC$ to envelop the Delta by the end of the millennium. The model of progress of religion from fetishism to theriomorphic (in the form of animals) polytheism to anthropomorphic polytheism to (true) monotheism should be set aside as a dangerously ethnocentric interpretation of the way that human beings seek to represent the forces of creation.

It is not often possible to suggest a reason why a particular place should adopt a particular deity as its local main focus of attention. On Elephantine the local goddess Satet may have a precise prehistoric link to the appreciation of the cavern under her shrine where the floodwaters could be heard just before the river surface itself began to rise; this might account for the restriction of her cult to that one place in Egypt. Another deity whose adoration at certain places can be explained is Sobek, the crocodile-god, the incarnation of the dreaded power to destroy that the

74

Egyptians encountered in the crocodile; at the parts of the river where marshes concealed animals or where difficult currents heightened the risk of shipwreck – in other words wherever the crocodile had the greatest opportunity for human catch – the attention of the local community naturally focused on Sobek, and his temples at Kom Ombo, Rizeiqat and the Fayum can be explained in this way. Despite the local voices for various deities, none of the different forms plays a role external to the patterns found in the pantheon that would be recognised throughout the country. Two forces are at work here, the need to mark off a distinctive form for specifically local worship as an expression of the local community, and the continued membership of a culture, a way of life, common to all living in the Nile Valley, speaking Egyptian and subject to Pharaoh. The interplay of these forces produces the range of the Egyptian pantheon and the transfers of identity, of role models, of patterns of relations and actions, from one place or one deity to another.

In each place, the deity took tangible form in its cult image, not in full identity but, according to the Egyptian texts, as a vessel in which the deity could rest and through which it could be given service and worship. The sacred bull of Ptah or that of Ra provided living variants of the same idea. This practice of denominating an object as a means of access to a deity created a paradox, that the image was present on earth and could be touched, but that it held divinity and ought not to be touched except under the most rigorous controls. Serving the image might involve the aspect of worship that is recognised in Christianity and Islam, that of praying to it and singing hymns to it; it might also stretch in ancient Egypt, unlike in Christianity and Islam, to more material service, to nourishment. Unlike the monotheistic creator-god, Egyptian deities were considered in need of verbal and material sustenance. Every day the image of the deity had to be provided with clean clothing, a morning meal and an evening meal; every morning, for this purpose, it was taken from a closed shrine, given fresh clothes and ornaments, to an accompaniment of incense-burning and chanting, and offered food and drink; every evening the reverse service would be performed, and the image returned behind the bolted doors of its shrine for the night, to rest until the next morning when the cycle would be repeated. The daily cult required an array of items, from the image itself and the shrine in which it was kept, to the altar or offering table and libation-vessel upon which the food and drink were placed, to the libation-vases for water and wine, and the arm-shaped censer for the burning of incense. The Egyptians did not construct large images of deities for the regular cult of each sanctuary, but instead marked the sanctity both by the small size or hidden-ness and by the precious materials of which it was made; accordingly the shrine too could be small enough to be portable, and would be made of rare wood set in precious metal, although larger enclosing shrines were also made of hard stone and, in exceptional instances, of great monoliths.

41 Representation of a man wearing the uraeus of kingship between two crocodiles, perhaps protectors of the king. Late Period, 4th century BC or later; linen, of unknown provenance. H. 47 cm. EA 10270.

The Egyptians named the temple of a deity its 'house' or 'estate', and the temple functioned like the estate of a nobleman, with the deity as its 'lord' present through the cult image, served by a staff and maintained by the income of fields and, in special cases, other sources; a stela at goldmines under Egyptian control in the south-eastern deserts records the decree of Sety I to divert the income of those mines to support his temple at Abydos, enjoining observance of the royal decree on all officials on pain of corporal punishment and criminal servitude. Most of the provincial temples are known only from later structures, and those of Lower and Middle Egypt have suffered particularly from the ravages of time and from their proximity to later centres of population eager to take for their own uses ready-quarried stone blocks. The former temples of Ptah at Memphis and of Atum at Iunu can scarcely be said to stand today even as ruins, so heavily have they been denuded of their limestone walls and hardstone statuary. Therefore our impression of an Egyptian temple is far from typical of the ancient range of types, and rests almost entirely on Upper Egyptian sites where the single model is the New Kingdom type at Thebes, taken up in the Ptolemaic Period for example at Edfu, where the temple of Horus remains one of the most perfectly preserved structures to survive from any land of antiquity.

The Theban model can be used to demonstrate the way in which the Egyptians wove into temple architecture their perception of the cosmos, but it should not be thought that quite the same method of symbolism was applied in every case. Common to all temples may be the notion of the temple as a manifestation of the primeval mound on which the sun-god stood at the dawn of existence. Thus the early temple at Medamud shares the feature of raised ground, although it should be noted that Medamud lies close to Thebes and may not prove early nationwide application of the principle. Theban temples differ from what may have been the earlier norm, if one existed, in a more external and far-reaching way, in their attention to the outside; the Theban temple is designed for festival, for approaching and acclaiming, and its architecture is absorbed to a large extent in the passage of ascent to the sanctuary. This incorporation of festival into temple architecture appears an innovation of the New Kingdom, precisely the period when temples began to expand to receive the largest share in output of monuments, a share taken in the Old and Middle Kingdoms by complexes for the cult of the king. The temple of Amun at Karnak, the central shrine of Thebes, had in the Middle Kingdom consisted of a rectangular sanctuary that was rebuilt and somewhat enlarged in limestone under Amenhotep I and Thutmose I; in the succeeding reigns it grew in the surrounding area until Amenhotep III transformed the entire East Bank at Thebes into a connected series of outwardly oriented temples as the setting for a great festival of state, the Ipet festival. His conception was enlarged under Ramses II, and their monumental ensemble is essentially what greets modern visitors to the site. In the Ipet festival the image of Amun was transported in a portable boat-shrine from Ipetsut, 'most favoured of places' – the Egyptian name for the Karnak temple – onto a full-size river boat that was then towed upstream to Ipetreset 'the private-chambers to the south' (modern Luxor). Ipetreset was dedicated to the cult of Amun in his form Kamutef, 'bull of his mother', signifying his role as progenitor of all creation. The passage for the festive procession seems to have been marked first by Hatshepsut, in whose reign so many features of Pharaonic civilisation took on new forms, but the temple complexes first formed an architectural unity embracing the Karnak temples of Amun and Mut and the Luxor temple of Amun under Amenhotep III.

In the Theban model exemplified by Karnak, Luxor and the West Bank temples for Amenhotep III and the Ramesside kings, the dominant feature is the pylon, a massive gateway that both heralds and conceals the shrine beyond, and is first attested at Karnak under Thutmose I. When oriented east-west as at Karnak and on the West Bank, the sun would rise or set between the twin towers of the pylon, evoking the hieroglyph for horizon in which the sun is portrayed between two hills. The solar focus was enhanced at Luxor and Karnak by a symbol borrowed from the sun temple at Iunu, the obelisk, a four-sided pillar surmounted by a pyramid

42 Censer for burning incense in temple ritual. Incense was indispensable in purifying and distinguishing the atmosphere around the divine image. The Egyptian censer took the form of a hand with outstretched palm bearing the vessel for the incense, while the other end was in the shape of a falcon head; this example has a centrepiece in the shape of a man proffering a libation bowl. Late Period, after 600 BC; bronze, of unknown provenance. L. 48.3 cm. EA 41606

43 Model shrine to be worn on a string, possibly for funerary rather than daily life or ritual. As in a full-size sanctuary, the divine image is concealed behind a series of doors and the outer chamber is surmounted by a winged sun-disk and frieze of uraei. In this model the sacred image is a head of a lioness, perhaps to represent the goddess Sekhmet, here shown with necklaces or garlands forming a semicircle beneath her head. Such motifs, given the name aegis by Egyptologists, adorned the ends of sacred boats and served to identify the deity of the boat. Late Period, after 600 BC; green glazed composition, of unknown provenance. H. 4.9 cm. EA 59402.

carved from a single block of Aswan granite and capped with gold; as the first ray of the sun reached from the horizon immediately before sunrise, it caught the metallic tip of the pyramid and caused it to shine in the twilight. Pylons were fronted by the shaped trunks of the tallest coniferous trees to carry tapering banners; in general two such flagstaffs about thirty metres tall were installed before a pylon, held in place by projections of wood from the upper part of the pylon face, but at Karnak the flagstaffs before the pylon numbered four and would have extended to sixty metres in height, towering over the pylon itself. Up to the sole and central gateway in the pylon led a broad avenue flanked, in East Thebes, by sphinxes. At the temple of Amun at Karnak the sphinxes do not have the head of the king but that of the ram, symbol of Amun. They were set up between the temple and the river quay to the west by Ramses II, and by Amenhotep III on the direct land-route from the temple toward Luxor temple. Other sphinx alleys include that between the Amun and Mut temples at Karnak, set up by Tutankhamun or his second successor Horemheb, and the avenue approaching the Amun temple at Luxor, set up by Nakhtnebef who had the head of the sphinx modelled more regularly as that of a king; the sphinxes in these avenues protect between their paws and under their chins an image of the reigning king. The entrance to a festive temple would not be complete without its statuary, which invariably showed the king on a colossal scale seated or striding; small sculpture at temple entranceways included the king as sphinx, that is with the body of a lion, offering a vase containing ointment – an image that combines the role of offering appropriate to the king at the temple with the protective power of the sphinx needed at doorways. The protection of the temple could also be expressed by a relief scene of the king smiting enemies, used on the outer faces of pylons from the time of Thutmose III to the Ptolemaic Period, and elaborated by Ramses II at Luxor and at his cult temple the Ramesseum on the West Bank at Thebes to the full pictorial and textual account of his prowess in the battle of Qadesh.

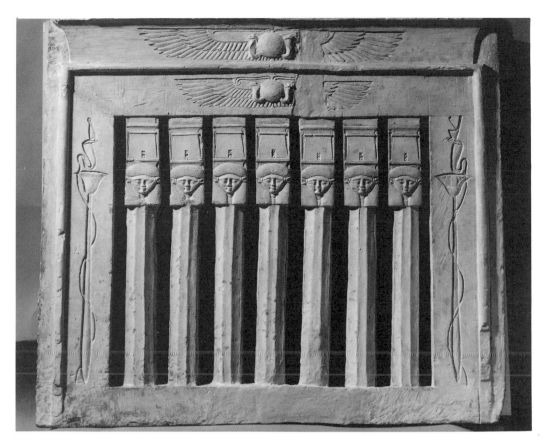

44 ABOVE A clerestory window with bars in the form of Hathor pillars, a cobra on each side to represent Upper and Lower Egypt and with the winged sun-disk in each border above. Such windows permitted limited light into the halls between the sunlit courts at the front of the temple and the lightless sanctuary at the back. Ptolemaic Period, 3rd century BC or later; limestone, said to be from Dendera. H. 19.7 cm. EA 1153.

45 RIGHT Column capital in the shape of a bundle of eight stems of papyrus, evoking the primeval marshes. The name in the upper cartouche is Amenhotep III, while those along the sides are Ramses II; the column itself has been dated on stylistic grounds to the Middle Kingdom. 12th Dynasty, c. 1900 BC (?); grey granite, found reused in a housewall in Cairo. H. (of entire column) 4.2 m. EA 64.

79

In the fourth century B C the wider area of the temple precinct was surrounded by a great wall of mud-brick, undulating like the waves of the primeval ocean Nun. This image of the temple as not only the house of a deity but more deeply as the primeval mound of creation then permeates the rest of the art and architecture in the sanctuary. Temple ceilings are adorned with stars or motifs of the sky goddess Nut, and temple walls and columns use the papyrus and lotus to summon up the atmosphere of primeval marshes; the lowest registers of walls often bear series of figures of Hapy, deity of the fertile flood, bringing the produce of the land for divine offerings. As the few allowed into the inner sanctum proceeded further and further toward the shrine of the deity each chamber had a higher floor level and a lower ceiling, making the ground rise like the mound of the first time, and the space around close further and further in on those present. From the outermost courtyard open to the sky with only a surrounding colonnaded corridor roofed over, the servants of the cult image moved into the half-lit inner colonnaded hall and then to the pitch-black holy of holies where the deity had space to rest in pure silence and lightlessness as in pre-existence. The decoration of the walls and the iconography of statues matched the change in tone; the outer courtyard might have columns with open floral capitals and statues of the king in the regalia of court ceremony, but the innermost hall would have columns with closed floral capitals and the image of the king cocooned in mummy-wrappings like Osiris, a chrysalis potent with life but waiting to unfurl. The contrast is drawn strikingly in the wayside temple built by Ramses III at what was then the threshold of the Amun temple at Karnak, but is now part of its enclosed first court. Such wayside temples for the portable bark-shrine of the god appear to be another innovation of Hatshepsut in the New Kingdom recasting of Egyptian temples; on its procession from one temple to the other, the bark of the god was given a wayside station at which to stop, called *wahet*, 'place for setting down'. Hatshepsut had six such shrines built between Karnak and Luxor for the Ipet festival, and others on the West Bank between the river and her own cult temple at Deir el-Bahri for the Valley festival.

To the modern onlooker an Egyptian temple of the most developed type, in particular the well-preserved Ptolemaic and Roman sanctuaries at Kom Ombo, Edfu and Dendera, may seem furnished with unbearably repetitive wall scenes of the king offering to the gods. Closer inspection reveals that no scene or detail is trivial, that the entire decorative programme has been put together according to specific rules, called by modern scholars the 'grammar of the temple', all of which serve to reinforce the central purpose of the structure as a means of preserving the universe through cult. In the great columned hall of Sety I and Ramses II at Karnak the scenes on the walls and columns follow a careful pattern in which each scene must complement those around it and those facing it directly and diagonally across the hall. Even the superficially mundane epithets of the king in cartouches throughout every scene in every part of the hall encode a very precise message; for example, the king is 'beloved of Ptah' along the route taken by offerings from the main temple to the small sanctuary of Ptah to the north, and from such examples the actual route of the staff in the daily life of the temple can eventually be reconstructed. Above all, the scenes of offering communicate a central message that the most casual observer could scarcely fail to miss: that the king alone can stand in the company of the gods, and that every offering is performed by the king. In practical experience the king would have carried out only an infinitesimal proportion of the total number of offerings made in his name, but the art on the walls perpetuated his direct offerings into eternity in stone, and still remind us that priests merely substituted for the king when they made offerings to gods and goddesses.

The pre-eminence of kingship in the surviving record should illustrate clearly that all cult in Egypt was royal cult; it was part of a cosmic pact in which the king offered up to heaven the fruits of the earth, in exchange channelling down to earth the blessings of heaven. Any temple in Egypt is a monument to the kingship that created it as much as to the deity for whom it was created. This softens the undeniable divide between the Old and Middle Kingdoms, when the craftshops of the state poured their material and human resources into constructing temple complexes for the cult of the reigning king, and the New Kingdom, Late Period and Ptolemaic Period, when the same craftshops devoted most of their efforts to constructing temples for the deities of localities. Since all monumental work in the name of a king contributed to the cult of that king, the change from one to the other focus of production is more one of form than of content; the emphasis passes from the image of the reigning king to the image of the local deity, but remains and depends on kingship. The substance of the change can better be appreciated by looking at temples for the cult of the reigning king, known from $c.3000-1150\,\mathrm{BC}$, than at temples for local deities which are poorly represented in the surviving record before the moment of change $c.1450\,\mathrm{BC}$. Such complexes are known to Egyptology as royal mortuary temples, implying that their main use was intended to follow the death of the king to whose cult they were dedicated. The evidence more strongly suggests that each king embarked on the construction of a temple for his own cult at the outset of his reign, that the temple would have been in operation during the reign, and that, far from coming into usage at the death of that king, the temple saw its income diverted and its cult begin to fall apart from the moment that he died and the new king sought to muster all possible resources for the benefit of his own new cult temple. The term 'mortuary temple' could therefore be replaced with the designation 'temple for the royal cult'; in Egyptian texts these temples are called from the late Middle Kingdom onwards 'temples of millions of years'.

The earliest known complexes for the cult of the king were rectangular enclosures of perishable materials, now vanished, marked out at Abydos near the border between desert and cultivation as spaces of unused ground amid the tombs of courtiers. From those tombs they may be dated to the first kings who ruled Egypt, whose burials lie not far distant to the west where the low desert sands nearest to the fields meet hillier Saharan terrain. Little is known of the tomb and cult complexes constructed for their successors, the kings who were buried at Saqqara, but one of the two kings who returned to Abydos for burial, Khasekhem(wy), left two great enclosures built of mud-brick instead of perishable material. One of these was at Abydos, removed from the tomb itself to the more accessible limit of cultivation like the earlier structures; the other stood in an entirely different location, near the ancient town of Nekhen (Hieraconpolis) where

Horus was worshipped in later times. The construction of similar edifices for the same king at different places prompted earlier Egyptologists to interpret both as 'forts' despite the military uselessness of both in planning and in location; it can instead be seen as an early instance of the rule made clear by later kings such as Ramses II that the cult of the king does not have to be confined to one place, and equally that it is not tied geographically just to the place where the king is to be buried. This is not to deny the special potency of the royal tomb as a magnet for the location of the royal cult; wherever the king was buried, there his cult would be in place, but the reverse did not apply. In the reigns after Khasekhem(wy) the royal burial place moved to Saqqara, and the cult temple for king Netjerkhet for the first time united the royal tomb with the royal cult, in the monumental stone complex of the Step Pyramid. From Netjerkhet to the late Middle Kingdom the main site of the royal cult stood at the royal tomb, classically in the pyramid complex as developed at Giza, with the pyramid towering behind as the solar focus of the cult, a temple

46 Fragment of the account from the pyramid and temple complex of king Neferirkara, with a duty-roster of men responsible at certain festivals for sacred emblems. The emblems are represented above the names of the men and on this fragment may be discerned as: baboon, scorpion, cobra, falcon-headed sphinx. 5th Dynasty, c. 2400 BC; papyrus, from Abusir. H. 20 cm. EA 10735, part.

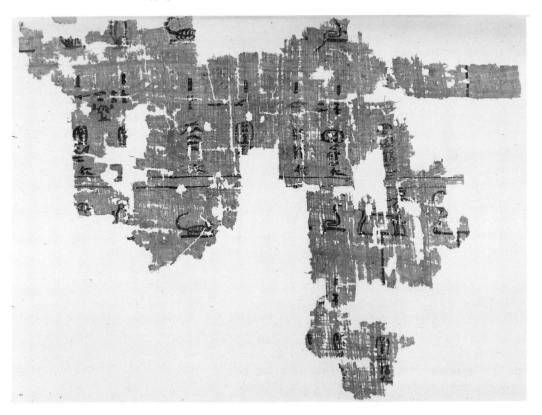

for the cult of the king at its eastern foot, a long causeway stretching down to the edge of the cultivation, and there a second temple.

The climax in the life of each complex would undoubtedly have been the funeral of the king for whom it was built; the funeral boat would have been greeted at the valley temple, where rites would have been performed before the body was borne up to the pyramid temple for further ceremonies, and then buried in its sarcophagus within the pyramid itself. As soon as the new reign began, the complex would have become second in importance to the new cult temple and pyramid of the successor; archaeologists were able in the excavation of the pyramid complex of Menkaura at Giza to reconstruct a pitiful picture of the fate of its temples, within a century or two reduced to a shabby group of houses for its staff, where the main industry, in the absence of regular income from agricultural estates, consisted of smashing the stone statues and vessels intended for the cult into small pieces suitable for the production of model vases, part of the contemporary burial equipment of officialdom. The papyrus archive of the temple of Neferirkara at Abusir reveals a similar picture of the slow evaporation of a cult after the death of its founder and beneficiary; the papyri comprise meticulous accounts of staff service, income from estates, and inspections of utensils employed in the cult, in the latter case noting more and more damage and less and less repair. The accounts papyri illustrate how such complexes could be afflicted so quickly when they had been set up by the most powerful person in the land for all eternity, for 'millions of years' as in the later phrase; income was diverted 'on paper' from one cult to another, in a system comparable to the paperwork in modern banking, and estates set up for one cult ended by supplying many destinations. The system was comparable to the 'reversion of offerings', the principle that allowed priests to partake of divine offerings after they had been placed before the cult image of the deity; in the instance of cults across a wide area, it would not have been practicable to send food and drink on a long journey through the countryside, particularly in the height of a hot summer, and the final destinations would have been calculated on paper. The more claimants on any one estate, the smaller the share and the greater the danger that the older cults would be bypassed completely. The only route of escape from this oblivion was the favour of a new king who could issue an edict exempting a particular cult from general obligations, or grant it new estates. Several such decrees survive from the Pyramid Age, but they testify as much to the struggle of such cults for survival as to the piety of the kings who issued them.

When after a century or more of disunity the governors of Thebes succeeded in reunifying Egypt under their control, they retained the family burial place at Thebes; the man who achieved reunification to become king of Egypt, Nebhepetra Mentuhotep, had his tomb and temple built on the West Bank at Thebes in the desert cliffs of Deir el-Bahri. His rock-cut tomb and shrine did not lie behind a court with columned façade, the type usual among his predecessors as Theban noblemen, but were instead concealed behind a massive square-based structure with colonnade and statues of the king mummiform with the regalia of the Two Lands. To the east a shaft led to a second burial chamber in which a statue of the king, face blackened like the fertile silt of Osiris, was wrapped in linen and buried

47 Stela representing four colossal statues at the temple of Nebhepetra Mentuhotep on the Theban West Bank. The outer figure on the right wears the Red Crown and is labelled as Nebhepetra, while the inner pair with the White Crown and the Double Crown are identified with the cartouches of Amenhotep I, and the left figure with the White Crown has no name on the surviving fragment. In accordance with the rules of Egyptian art the faces are shown in profile and the shoulders frontally, although the surviving colossal statues face ahead not to the side. Amenhotep I added to the work of Nebhepetra Mentuhotep two generations before Hatshepsut's spectacular terraced temple was constructed alongside and shifted the focus of cult north from the Nebhepetra sanctuary. 18th Dynasty, c. 1500 BC; limestone, from Deir el-Bahri, Thebes. H. 30 cm. EA 690.

as a second tomb for the royal spirit. The provision of a second chamber occurred already in the Step Pyramid of Netjerkhet, and in the classic pyramid complex a subsidiary pyramid could also be provided for the same purpose; as in other funerary customs the principle of substitution held more vital force for the Egyptians than it may do for us, and a correctly formed and appointed substitute could with the proper rites take the place of the body itself, for example if the body was damaged or destroyed by violators of the burial. The temple of Mentuhotep became the principal Middle Kingdom monument on the West Bank at Thebes, and the 'ferrying to the valley of Nebhepetra' of Amun of Karnak set up a model followed in the New Kingdom, when the 'beautiful feast of the valley' saw the Amun image escorted over the river from Karnak to the West Bank for a visit to at least the temple of the reigning king and perhaps to each of the then functioning royal cult temples. The festival took place in the third month of summer, and gave an opportunity to all Thebans to celebrate with their dead relatives on the West Bank. The temple of Nebhepetra also appears in the texts as a temple of Amun, and each temple to the royal cult saw a similar identification; at Thebes each royal cult temple housed a cult to Amun, whereas the valley temple of Senusret II at Lahun was called in its own archive a temple of Anubis.

Kings of the late Middle Kingdom, early New Kingdom and Ramesside Period, as mentioned in the previous chapter, founded a series of temples for the royal cult at Abydos where the tomb of Djer had been reinterpreted as the burial place of Osiris. The most elaborate of these so-called false tombs or 'cenotaphs' (modern commentators have thought to insist that only the royal burial place could attract the temple for the eternal cult of a king) is that of Sety I. The temple of Sety I contained a series of seven chapels instead of the usual one, and that of Osiris led through to a separate shrine of three chapels for Osiris-Sety I, Isis and Horus; the other six chapels housed the cult images for Isis, Horus, Amun-Ra, Ra-Horakhty, Ptah and, again, Sety I. To the south a separate corridor opened to a columned hall before the shrines of Ptah-Sokar and Nefertem; a parallel corridor led past a list of all previous kings to whom offerings were given in the temple, up a corridor to the desert reach behind, where a second more mysterious structure lay concealed beneath the sand. This second edifice in the complex consisted of a central columned hall surrounded by a lower passage flooded by the Nile, with a sarcophagus chamber at the far end; the hall was entered by a sloping corridor the walls of which were inscribed in the reign of Merenptah, grandson of Sety I, with excerpts from funerary texts and scenes of offerings. The ceiling of the sarcophagus chamber bears one of the earliest representations of the sky Nut held aloft by Shu, a scene accompanied here by descriptions of the various corners of the cosmos. The extraordinary plan and contents of the Abydos precinct of Sety I may be explained in part by the place of the reign in history, barely a generation after the death of Akhenaten and the subsequent return to traditional religious expression; in Abydos Sety I reaffirmed the role of Osiris and the offerings to previous kings, two features that had been swept aside or largely forgotten in the reforms of Akhenaten. The introduction of the cult of Sety I to the place where Osiris was believed to have been buried continued a practice that had been in force before the reign of Akhena-

85

ten, and it provided an opportunity to formulate traditional belief explicitly on stone, both in texts and in two-dimensional representation.

The New Kingdom had already seen a looser connection between burial place and cult centre with the decision to bury the sovereign in the Theban mountain while siting the temple on the edge of the cultivation below, a decision taken perhaps under Amenhotep I although first securely attested for Hatshepsut. In this arrangement the kings reverted, probably unwittingly, to the model of the early dynastic kings at Abydos; it is only vaguely conceivable that the late Middle and early New Kingdom activity at Abydos opened the eyes of royal planners to the possibility of dividing burial place from temple, as was done there for Osiris. Unless she was taking over work begun by her father Thutmose I and her half-brother and spouse Thutmose II, Hatshepsut had built for herself both a tomb in the Valley of the Kings and a terraced temple at the end of the valley of Deir el-Bahri. Keen to legitimate her syntactically difficult claim to be a female Horus, Hatshepsut had inscribed what are now the earliest surviving royal copies of such fundamental statements of kingship as the *King as Priest of the Sun* and the divine birth of the king. The terraced temple was inspired by the adjacent temple for the cult of Nebhepetra Mentuhotep but it transcended its model by marrying the terraces to the side of the desert cliff behind and expanding the number of terraces and shrines upon them. Among the extraordinary features are the coloured reliefs depicting the transport of monolithic obelisks from the Aswan granite quarries and the despatch and return of an expedition to a forested Red Sea land identified as Punt from which the Egyptians procured exotic raw materials, in particular incense. In the succeeding reigns the name of Hatshepsut was erased and the temple became a sanctuary solely for its other deities, Amun, Anubis and Hathor; the successors of Hatshepsut were unable to match her magnificence until the accession of Amenhotep III. The temple of the latter is now a wasteland stretching between two of the more remarkable sights of Thebes, a great stela that would have stood near the sanctuary, and the two colossal statues of the king enthroned that flanked the entrance to the complex; the desolation seems the more complete for the existence of the inscription that describes it as the most brilliant of the many brilliant accomplishments of the gold-rich reign.

Amenhotep III was no longer-lived at Memphis where he had constructed another temple for his own cult at the precinct of the temple of Ptah; it has vanished entirely, and even its location cannot be determined, although the Egyptologist Robert Morkot has presented persuasive grounds for identifying it as the main Ptah temple presently visible at the site. Outside Thebes the work of the king in perpetuating his cult has survived most solidly in Nubia, where small shrines to the cult of the conquerors Senusret III and Thutmose III already existed; Amenhotep III overshadowed these with the scale of his work above all at Soleb and Sedeinga,

48 Head from a colossal statue of Amenhotep III from his cult temple on the West Bank at Thebes; the features anticipate the radical change in art under Akhenaten. 18th Dynasty, *c.* 1350 BC; quartzite, from Thebes. H. 1.17 m. EA 7.

the former a temple to his own cult, the latter emphasising the role of his principal queen Tiy. In statuary too the king surpassed all his predecessors; visitors to the Egyptian Museum in Cairo still witness the statue of the royal couple enthroned towering over every other colossal statue in the central hall of the building, and the head and arm of another statue of the king from the temple of Mut is housed in the British Museum, where even in one of the tallest galleries it would not fit had it not lost the greater part of its body. In front of the temple at Soleb Amenhotep III extended the symbol of the sphinx as an image of sovereign power to identify himself fully with the lion, and had a pair of Aswan granite lions flank the entrance; they were removed by a Kushite king several centuries later to the temple of Amun at Gebel Barkal where they marked the path from the ceremonial palace toward the sacred mountain there. Despite the varied history of the pair, neither being finished and both being moved, one still bears the identifying label 'the lion great of strength, beloved of Amun-Ra'. In all these monuments the king is stepping beyond the bounds of what had been achieved to mark his own divinity with unique force and splendour.

The relative modern ignorance of Amenhotep III may be attributed to his successors. His son Akhenaten sought to push the theological conflict of the day to the utmost, and to build on as vast a scale as his father; then the child Tutankhamun captured modern imagination not for the immense programme of restoration that was launched in the wake of Akhenaten but for the historical accident that the gold of his burial survived; the following century brought with a new dynasty another king with a mission to immortalise himself, Ramses II. Many of the monuments of Amenhotep III fell as quarries to the Ramesside builders; his cult temple at Memphis may have disappeared to construct the cult temple of Ramses II at the same site as Robert Morkot suggests, and his primary cult temple at Thebes became the building stones for the cult temple of Merenptah, successor of Ramses II. In part this may have been due to the destructive work of Akhenaten, whose agents did not spare the monuments of his father in their frenzy to destroy the name of Amun everywhere in Egypt and Nubia. It also seems that Amenhotep III suffered from being too perfect a role model; the sites he chose were expanded by Ramses II, as at Luxor where the Amun temple was doubled in size, and at Karnak where the columned hall that still dominates the temple was completed, and even the colossal statuary of the king was taken over and remodelled, as the Egyptologist Arielle Kozloff has shown in the case of such works as the British Museum colossal head. Yet Ramses II also had built monuments of not just staggering size but extraordinary originality; the temples for his cult include, beside his main complex at Thebes – known today as the Ramesseum – the Abydos temple cited above, the depleted ruins of his temple at Memphis, so vast that it is now somewhat misleadingly named the Great Temple of Ptah, the vanished cult centres of Iunu (Heliopolis), his new Residence Per-Ramses in the Eastern Delta, and his extraordinary series of temples in Nubia. Of these Nubian temples, those at Wadi el-Sebua, Gerf Hussein and Derr were allotted to the administrations of the temples of Amun, Ptah and Ra respectively, as if to mirror in Nubia the royal building programme within Egypt. The most celebrated of the Nubian temples is the Abu

Simbel complex, a pair of rock temples, one for the cult of the king alongside Amun, Ra and Ptah, the other highlighting his queen Nefertari in the role of Hathor, reminiscent of the two temples of Amenhotep III at Soleb and Sedeinga. The international coordination and expertise required to move the temples out of the reach of the new lake created by the building of the Aswan High Dam allowed modern observers to appreciate in detail the work and precision of the ancient builders that allowed an alignment so perfect that twice a year the sun penetrated to the innermost sanctuary of the main temple and illuminated at dawn the rock-cut cult image of the king.

Among the temples for his own cult and those he constructed for other deities, Ramses II included texts and depictions of the battle of Qadesh, a titanic conflict in which the king almost lost his life. Commentators often chide Ramses II for celebrating a near-defeat, but they are not in tune with the purpose of the record, which is not to celebrate a military victory, but to perpetuate a moment in which the reigning king fulfilled a part of the repertoire of kingship. The battle of Qadesh saw the king escape death by leading a sally out of encirclement, and thereby revealing himself as initiator of action in the defence of Right. About two centuries earlier Thutmose III experienced the same fulfilment when he led his troops through a narrow pass and took his enemies by surprise at Megiddo, again an example not of military victory, for a long, exhausting and unnecessary siege ensued, but of the king as champion of order like Horus and initiator of action like Ra. The exceptional cosmic character of the Qadesh incident explains why court artists devised such unprecedentedly elaborate compositions to celebrate the event, and why it was repeated on temple walls and recorded in literary manuscripts. A century later Ramses III found himself in the same position again, with an invasion from north and west, by land and water; his successful resistance did not prevent large-scale immigration, but the role of king as champion of order brought a new outpouring of artistry in unique representations of ship-battles on the outer walls of his cult temple at Medinet Habu on the Theban West Bank.

The temple at Medinet Habu is the principal recipient of royal largesse on one of the most often cited and least understood of the remarkable documents that survive from Pharaonic Egypt, known as the Great Harris Papyrus after its first modern owner and now in the British Museum (EA 9999). The papyrus extends to over 40 m, one of the longest surviving manuscripts, and contains three sections in which Ramses III records the vast estates that he offered the gods of Thebes, Memphis and Iunu (Heliopolis). Usually it is cited as an example of the loss of royal power to the temples, because so much land is given that it would leave most of the country in the hands of the priests. However, this document is a product not of the reign of Ramses III but of his son Ramses IV, and each section of the papyrus focuses on an appeal to the relevant deities to secure the accession of Ramses IV, reinforced by a coloured full-height illustration showing the deified Ramses III addressing the gods of first Thebes, then Memphis, and finally Iunu. The special circumstance is revealed by another series of papyri which show that not everyone feared Pharaoh as a god, namely the record of trials of the assassins of Ramses III; although conspirators were tried and convicted, the succession required special

89

pleading with the gods, and in this atmosphere the records of royal donations by Ramses III were amassed into a single document that constituted a prayer by Ramses IV for a smooth transfer of power to himself.

The Egyptologist Eric Uphill has shown that the donations by Ramses III are not to the old temples or their priesthoods, but overwhelmingly to new temples that stood on the precincts of particular deities but were dedicated to the cult of the reigning king, Ramses III. Foremost among these ranked the temple at Medinet Habu, the most impressive surviving monument of the king or any of his sons and successors. Another Theban temple which also survives is the wayside shrine now in the first court of the Amun temple at Karnak. The papyrus cites in addition the great temples of the king at Memphis (possibly a simple renewal of the temple of Ramses II there, since the cartouches of the king are among the few later marks of royal interest in that site) and Iunu, as well as a sanctuary in Palestine. As Eric Uphill notes, the officials in charge of the new foundations for the royal cult with the vast estates to support them are not priests but officials at the royal court. It seems that the extraordinary feature of the donations by Ramses III is not that they were made but that they were recorded, a feature that can be explained by the astonishing circumstances following the conspiracy against his life. If Medinet Habu required such massive support from estates throughout the country, the same can probably be assumed for the colossal monumental output of Ramses II, Amenhotep III and before them the builders of the pyramids. The diversion of royal offerings thus becomes easier to understand as an act not so much of impiety as of stark necessity, and the cycle of building and diverting funds becomes more clearly visible in the record. The act of building, though claimed for the future, is always an act in, for and on the terms of the present, like the modern custom of setting up a tombstone in cemeteries full of the fallen tombstones of previous years; the ancient like the modern monument was set up to fulfil a need in its present time, whether the cult of king or gods or the dead.

The meaning of royal works in their own times can best be approached through the festival of kingship, recorded in episodic scenes from the time of the first unification c. 3000 BC to the last use of Pharaonic art in the decoration of temple walls under Roman emperors of the second century AD. In contrast to European tradition the main festival of kingship was not the coronation, and indeed no exact parallel to a coronation can be cited from Egyptian sources; instead the festivals of kingship were of confirmation of power, at the New Year and most importantly at intervals of many years. Since three denotes the plural in Egyptian script and art, an interval of three years, or more impressively three times ten = thirty years, gave the perfect timing for the renewal of royal power, understood as the exercise of power by the sun-god on earth. The festival of rejuvenation after a period of years, ideally thirty, was called the *sed*-festival, translated in Greek texts as the 'festival at thirty-year intervals'. *Sed* is the Egyptian word for 'tail' but it is unclear to what it refers in this context, if it is not the bull's tail shown at the back of the royal kilt to denote his creative force in potency. The *sed* is one of the first festivals to be recorded, in scenes on labels to mark the year of reign of early kings. The same scenes recur throughout Egyptian history, notably on a massive granite shrine

49 Flask for water from the rising Nile at the beginning of the flood, marking the start of the New Year. The goddess represented as a cow on the side of the flask may be Mehytweret, 'the great flood', rather than Hathor; the inscriptions along the side invoke Amun-Ra and Isis for a good new year. These vessels seem to appear no earlier than the seventh century BC, possibly inspired by foreign vase shapes. Late Period, after 600 BC; green glazed composition, of unknown provenance. H. 13 cm. EA 24651. Drawn by Christine Barratt.

constructed for the *sed* of Osorkon II in the ninth century BC at Bubastis. Although the internal order and significance of the festival ceremonies remain unclear in details, the principal events included the enthronement of the king twice on a raised stepped dais sheltered by a columned overhanging; the two enthronements, once with the Red Crown and once with the White Crown, were the subject of the hieroglyph used to write the name of the festival, showing both scenes back to back under the same double canopy. The Red and White Crowns came to be aligned on monuments with symbols of Lower and Upper Egypt respectively, at least from the reign of Amenhotep III, but this may be a reinterpretation. Red represents the danger of blood, as in the *tit*-amulet of red jasper said, in the funerary text for its making, to be the blood of Isis; it could also be used as the colour of the sun-disk in coloured two-dimensional depictions. White is acclaimed in the texts as the colour of brightest sunlight and of purity. The prototypes of the two crowns and their colouring are lost in the sparse record for the fourth millennium BC, but their hue at least may focus more on the oppositions of purity and power; thus the crowns may belong inextricably together rather than prove the existence of two opposing kingdoms *c.* 3000 BC joined in the original process of unification. When the two crowns were first paired, their shapes might have been adapted, which would explain why they fit together so well and may account for the strange shape of the Red Crown.

50 Label once attached to a container or oil on which the owner's name, an official, appears on the left side. On the right the year of production (?) is identified with the tall hieroglyph for 'year' on the outside and the main event of the year, a kingship festival. King Den is shown wearing the Double Crown, seated in a pavilion on a stepped platform, and running a course marked by semicircular stones. 1st Dynasty, c.3000 BC; ebony, from the tomb of Den at Abydos. H. 5.5 cm. EA 32650.

Of the other episodes of the *sed* the most frequently depicted are perhaps those in which the king runs four courses in the presence of deities, holding a batch of documents, an oar, or the more familiar insignia of shepherd's crook and the flail. These courses may, as usually surmised, reflect a prehistoric endurance test to be sure that the ruler was still fit and able, but in Pharaonic times they seem to present the king after the rites of the festival already rejuvenated, more a demonstration than a test of royal vigour. Rejuvenated, the king was able to continue like the sun after sunrise at the height of his powers.

Distinct from the *sed* stands a kingship ritual preserved upon a broken papyrus of *c*. 1800 BC in which the king cited is not the reigning sovereign but Senusret I who lived two centuries earlier. The text is written in cursive hieroglyphs as if it were the original roll held by the officiant in the ceremonies, and the ritual may have been performed by Senusret I for the installation of his additions to the Amun temple at Karnak. Since his Amun temple remained the principal monumental complex at Karnak until Amenhotep I and his successors began to transform the site, a ritual of Senusret I might have been re-enacted in later generations, or at least have remained an efficacious text in the library of temple or priest. (The work of Amenhotep I for Amun may similarly have led to the inclusion of the king in the daily cult routine at Karnak, as shown in the Amun temple ritual papyri of Ramesside date.) In the kingship ritual of Senusret I, a *djed*-pillar was raised and the king received symbols of his office, in particular a double-plumed crown.

A fourth-century BC papyrus preserves another ancient ceremony: the confirmation of royal power at the end of each year, when the forces of chaos threatened to overturn order and the inheritance of Horus, that is Pharaoh's kingship, had to be reconfirmed. This and other ceremonies of the triumph of kingship became regular festivals at the temple of Horus in Edfu, but the papyrus puts the New Year preparations in their original royal setting. The New Year in Egypt marked the start of the summer flood, around mid-July according to our calendar, a time when all Egyptians would anxiously wait to see if the flood rose enough to water the fields or too much so that it swept away topsoil and even buildings and animals. In those days the rituals for the assertion of the royal and divine order attained paramount importance, symbolised in a ceremony that is recorded in Ptolemaic temple texts and architecture. The ceremony was performed on the first day of the first month, the Opening of the Year, also called Birth of Ra; it culminated in a procession escorting the sacred images of the deities worshipped in the temple, leading up to a chapel on the roof. There the statue could 'see' and 'join' the sun-disk; this action activated the statue so that the ba-spirit of the deity could see, hear and act through the earthly vehicle of the statue.

The New Year ceremony may be the main reason for the existence of solar sanctuaries at Abu Simbel and Karnak, and it demonstrates the solar underpinning of Egyptian cult. Surviving solar sanctuaries, with courtyards open to the rays of the sun and altars where offering could be made in the sunlight, certainly differ from the covered dark world of temples on the Theban model. The most famous sun temples are the great shrines built by Akhenaten in his city Akhetaten for the sun-disk. These lavish structures may not be as revolutionary as our familiarity with surviving Upper Egyptian temples might suggest; the temples of the sun at Iunu may have provided a direct model, and solar sanctuaries of the twenty-sixth century BC at Abu Gurab already point to different architectural possibilities for cult, in their open courts and the massive bulk of their 'obelisks', evoking the primeval benben-stone.

The New Year ceremony of 'joining the sun-disk' recalls strikingly the Tale of Sanehat in which the death of the king is described as union with the sun-disk. This connects solar and royal cult, but it also directs us to a feature that lasts the length of ancient Egyptian history, the activation of the statue. In Egyptian phrasing the mouth of the statue was opened by a special rite in which a priest touched the image at the lips with special tools. The same rites were performed on temple and tomb-chapel statuary, and at least in later periods on mummies or anthropoid coffins, and tombs of both nobles and kings included the sequence of ceremonies in fuller or shorter versions in the decoration of their tomb-chapels and burial chamber walls. In the late third millennium miniature sets of tools for the ceremony were included in burial equipment as part of the means for surviving death; according to an inscription of Amenemhat II in the nineteenth century BC, a 'fully equipped chest for opening the mouth' formed a part of temple apparel and a papyrus of the second century AD preserves the ritual, evidence of its continued role down to that latest period in ancient Egyptian textual traditions. The rite of 'opening the mouth' aimed at bringing life not to but via an inanimate representation of a person or deity. Without the opening of the mouth, the image could not be home to the spirit and allow it to benefit from the faculties of human existence, above all the ability of the ka-spirit to consume offerings brought for its sustenance. Every Egyptian statue upon which the rite had been performed ceased to be a block of stone or wood and became a vessel for the spirit; every image with an offering text continues in the ancient Egyptian approach to sustain whoever it portrays.

Given the notion of the vital statue, the priest performed in essence the functions of a household servant, feeding, cleaning, clothing and escorting the image of the deity as well as managing its revenues. There is little evidence for people occupied entirely in priestly duties before the twenty-sixth century BC; priestly titles of the previous centuries in the written record belong to men whose main tasks lay within the royal administration. In the twenty-sixth century we have the first evidence for the operation of a royal cult temple, from the survival of archives of papyrus at the royal cult temples in Abusir; these reveal a rota system by which the temple staff of all levels, manual and clerical, divided into five 'watches', each of which had to supply temple staff for one month after which the next guard would take over temple duties. In this system no man could serve more than three months a year; at each change of guard all the property in the temple was checked for damage and the results registered on papyrus, to enable the authorities to determine responsibility for any losses. Income and expenditure as well as priestly duties in the cult were also all meticulously recorded as long as the infrastructure of the temple estate survived. It is not known whether the same intricate system was to be found at all temples or only at those for the royal cult. Both royal and local cult temples might be granted exemption by royal decree from the onerous obligations to support royal works as occasion demanded; the need for special exemption suggests that normally the temples were bound to give whatever was required of them by officials of the king, whether manpower or goods in kind. In the late third and early second millennia it became the norm for local governors to take the title 'overseer of priests', further reinforcing the external control over the temples and their revenues. It may be noted that the late third millennium is the only period in which many women held priestly titles; at other periods their role seems confined to the function of making music as accompaniment to the cult of a deity.

From the eighteenth century BC survives one particularly rich source, the business archive of a temple scribe Horemsaf who served at the royal cult temple of Senusret II at Sekhemsenusret (near the modern village Lahun). Alongside the accounts so familiar from the Abusir archive, his archive includes correspondence

51 Stela of Neferaabet with funerary representations and texts. The text at the bottom describes 'descending to the tribunal of Osiris' from the *Book of the Dead*; above it appears Anubis at work on mummifying the deceased, while the top register depicts mourners around the scene of the 'opening the mouth' for four mummies. The rite is performed by a son of the deceased with an adze-shaped tool under the directions of a lector-priest, shown behind the mummies reading from the papyrus roll containing the correct procedures for the funeral. 19th Dynasty, *c.*1250 BC; limestone, from Deir el-Medina, Thebes. H 63 cm. EA 305.

52 and 53 Once its mouth had been 'opened' in the prescribed manner each statue became empowered to receive the sustenance of food for the being that it depicted. The Ramesside statue here would have been fed from appointed estates as documented in the papyrus illustrated below it, an account for 'grain of the statue of Ramses-beloved-of-Amun' from an estate in Middle Egypt. Food and drink offerings would 'revert' to other cults and finally to the temple staff. STATUE 19th Dynasty, $c.$ 1250 BC (?); granite; of unknown provenance. H 56 cm. EA 125. PAPYRUS 19th Dynasty, $c.$ 1225 BC; papyrus, of unknown provenance. H 12 cm. EA 10447.

with the governor of the town in the capacity of overseer of priests. The number of watches at the temple was four, and not every member of a guard served each of the three times a year that it was required to supply staff. As at Abusir, service involved working within the temple, the separate term 'men in front of the fields' being used for work on the estates outside the temple precinct. In the New Kingdom there is less evidence for the system of 'guards' of staff, although no records comparable to the Abusir and Lahun archives have survived from this period. At the same time the role of priest seems to have become more full-time and is cited in literary papyri among professions like scribe, soldier and farmer. The priest described by scribes in a satirical vein is not a privileged member of society, being forced to perform the service three times a day. This may be true at the lower end of the scale, but the career of Bakenkhons in the thirteenth centy BC gives a more precise picture, as recorded on his two statues. After four years in the 'chamber of schooling' of the Mut temple, Bakenkhons became a stable official, a post at which he remained for eleven years before his priestly career opened with four years as 'pure-priest', followed by twelve years as 'god's father', fifteen years as the third 'god's servant' and twelve years as the second 'god's servant' before his appointment as high priest, all in the service of Amun. A high priest of Amun was responsible not only for cult and revenues of the vast enterprise that was Karnak but also, at least in the case of Bakenkhons, building work in the precincts.

Although priestesses are rare after the Old Kingdom, queen Ahmose Nefertari of the sixteenth century BC attained an exceptional position as second 'god's servant' of Amun, a post that she exchanged under contract, recorded on a stela at Karnak, for the new title 'wife of the god' or 'adoratrice of the god'. In the first millennium BC this post became more important than that of high priest, and was used by the Kushite kings of the eighth and seventh centuries and their Saite successors into the sixth century to cement royal control over Thebes; each 'god's wife' was celibate in this later period, and had to adopt her successor, usually the daughter of the reigning king. At the change of dynasty from Kushite to Saite, with the Assyrian invasions in the background, the adoption of the Saite princess Neitiqret by the old Kushite 'god's wife' allowed a smooth transfer of power at national level, and was recorded on another Karnak stela. The last Saite 'god's wife', Ankhnesneferibra, had prepared for her burial at least as far as commissioning the magnificent sarcophagus with its unique series of funerary texts, but the Persians invaded Egypt, and nothing is known of her fate. The title of 'god's wife' seems to have survived the invasion, but the office receded in importance and no later holder can even be named. In part the history of the 'god's wife of Amun' runs the opposite course to that of high priest; between Ahmose Nefertari and the Kushite installation of Amenirdis, the 'god's wife' seems less prominent while the high priest played a powerful role, most clearly seen in the person of Amenhotep during the reigns of Ramses IX and X, in which time he was first removed and then regained office. The case of Amenhotep indicates both the power of the office and its military weakness. The most effective among high priests at exercising control over Thebes were the generals who took the title of high priest, first Herihor in the reign of Ramses XI, and then Payankh in the same reign; the king in the north saw authority divided

54 LEFT Figure of the god's wife Ankhnesneferibra on her sarcophagus, reused in the Roman Period and found without a burial in the last century. She is represented in the long robe and sandals of her day, wearing a vulture headdress with uraeus and, to reinforce her share in the sovereignty of the sun-god, horned sun-disk with double plumes. She holds the crook and flail. 26th Dynasty, *c*.550 BC; schist, from Thebes. H. of full sarcophagus 2.57 m. EA 32, detail.

55 OPPOSITE Stela of Pasebakha(en)nuit, a priest of Min of Coptos and son of the high priest of Amun-Ra. He is shown offering to Osiris, behind whom appear Horus and Isis. Traces reveal that the priest was originally offering a figure of the goddess Right (Maat), but this has been erased and replaced by a crudely drawn *tit*-knot amulet, presumably because only the king was supposed to offer Right to the gods. Shortly after this stela was set up, a new line of kings in the north reasserted authority over the Theban high priests, and the emendation may date to this change. Third Intermediate Period, *c*.950 BC; limestone, from Abydos. H. 91.4 cm. EA 642.

between the general/high priest in the south and in the north a man of unknown origin named Nesbanebdjed (rendered later as Smendes by the Greeks). This arrangement was at first hailed as a new era of 'repeating of births' i.e. renaissance. The successors of Nesbanebdjed kept the kingship, while the successors of Payankh retained the position of high priest; the harmonious accord ended only in the tenth century BC when a family of Libyan origin came to power and took the precaution of making a royal prince the high priest.

The influence of the high priest is thought to have lain in the custom, prominent from c. 1450 BC to the Roman Period and particularly at Thebes, of solving questions by recourse to the oracle. In practice the decisions of the Amun oracle concerned high affairs of state, and it is difficult to imagine that these, any more than temple revenues, fell outside the sphere of action of the king, at least so long as the kings interested themselves in Thebes. The first instance of an oracle is that recorded by Hatshepsut when the voice of Amun legitimated her own all but untenable position as female king. More mundane affairs of daily life tended to be directed at more accessible deities, such as the patrons of the West Bank at Thebes, King Amenhotep I and his mother Ahmose Nefertari. In Egypt oracles usually took place during festivals when the image of the deity was being transported in its small portable bark-shrine outside its temple; questions could then be put to the oracle, generally as alternative 'yes/no' documents between which the god had to choose by moving his bark. The opportunities for abuse seem to us legion, but the practice provided an avenue for settling legal disputes within a socially recognised framework, avoided more difficult cases degenerating into violence and lawlessness and gave speedy results. A measure of state control of abuse was ensured by the state officials who took part in the procedures. The Egyptians themselves did not always accept the verdict of an oracle; in one late Ramesside papyrus now in the British Museum a certain Patjauemdiamen takes his case to no fewer than three forms of Amun before confessing guilt of theft. Thus the oracle became another legal recourse beside the civil courts that alone had been available before Hatshepsut, an example of the world becoming less rather than more secular.

Abuse of priestly position was not confined to the possibilities opened by the custom of the oracle. A famous petition of the sixth century BC by a priest called Padiaset (often rendered Petiese by Egpytologists) concerns mismanagement and even violent persecution of the plaintiff at his local temple, and the petitions of one Hor in the second century BC give details of negligence in feeding the sacred ibis flocks to the point where the birds are said to be starving. Even allowing for rhetoric, the recurrent legal cases from Ramesside times on do not inspire confidence, and yet it may be unwise to attribute this corruption to a priestly class; in much of the preceding it can be seen that priests were another set of officials and workers, distinguished only by working for a temple, and corruption in temples had its equal in other departments of the administration. Only in the Ptolemaic and Roman Periods do the priests seem to form a separate class, but in those centuries all other branches of officialdom fell into the hands of Hellenes, leaving the temple priesthood as the last group of Egyptian titleholders. In the third century BC priests even began to issue decrees to promulgate the royal cult, a prerogative of Pharaoh that would never have been ceded had the Macedonian rulers been able to communicate in Egyptian as well as Greek. One such decree is that for the cult of Ptolemy v, a boy-king whose forces were fighting rebellion in the Delta and the complete secession of Upper Egypt, a dramatic text of kingship but one most widely known today because one copy in both Greek and Egyptian scripts prompted the way toward the decipherment of hieroglyphs, the Rosetta Stone.

The most distinct groups of priestly or temple workers were those with the specialised knowledge indispensable for conducting rites. Three key institutions sheltered the necessary learning and its implementation, the 'house of gold', the 'house of books' and the 'house of life'. The house of gold was the place where images were finished by the state craftsmen on the guidelines of Egyptian canonical art, and then transformed into potential vehicles for the spirit by the ceremony of opening the mouth. Both craftsmen and ritual officiants here kept alive the hieroglyphic kernel of Pharaonic civilisation. The house of books or 'library' played a similar role in perpetuating textual memory, a role exemplified in the library of the Osiris temple at Abydos; king Neferhotep of the eighteenth century BC consulted that library when preparing the commission for a new statue of Osiris, and fourth-century BC papyri cite the same source as home to the thousand-year-old manuscripts containing the texts of 'transfigurations' to be used for the murdered Osiris and, on the same model, all dead persons. The house of life is the name given to a building, as stamped in hieroglyphs on its bricks, near the state records office at Akhetaten. It also occurs as an institution of state in the Old Kingdom and as a place for storing texts and disseminating knowledge to initiates in the New Kingdom. In the fourth century BC a text ascribes it a role in the cult of Osiris and thus in the ritual of mummification where it is a stone-walled enclosure within which a pavilion housed an image of Osiris to be fashioned in the ceremonies. A second fourth-century BC text gives the pavilion of the house of life an equally crucial role in the ritual for confirming royal power at the New Year. By combining the function of a library with the role of keeping king and gods in action, the house of life acted as the underpinning of life itself in Egypt; without the sacred books there could be no ritual, and the core of the culture would vanish; without the cult the very fabric of the universe would be in danger of disintegration as human kind lost its ties to the world in which it lives.

The titles of priests often cloak the corresponding and equally crucial role of the personnel needed to maintain these core institutions. The high priest of Amun held no special title other than the simple 'first god's servant of Amun', perhaps because the cult came into existence only at the beginning of the second millennium. By contrast the high priest of the sun at Iunu held the principal title 'greatest of seers', a reference to the overarching visual bias of the solar cult, while the high priest of Thoth at Khemenu was designated 'great one of the five', referring to the creator and the four aspects of pre-existence, and the high priest of Ptah at Memphis was called 'greatest of directors of craftsmen', an early administrative title transposed to the cult of Ptah as god of crafts. By the end of the third millennium BC the high priest of Ptah also held the title *se(te)m*, an archaic title that brings us to central rites, above all the ceremony of opening the mouth; the *se(te)m* performed the role

56 Stela of Keh, a superintendent of the stores of offerings to Amun. Although his position was administrative, he is shown here in priestly mode with a bald head and wearing a panther skin; he pours a libation and burns incense at the offering-table of Osiris. Behind Osiris are seen the West, the land of tombs personified as a goddess, and the god Anubis. In the bottom two registers, Keh himself receives offerings from his family. 19th Dynasty, *c*.1250 BC; painted limestone, from Abydos (?). H. 66 cm. EA 303.

of son for father, Horus to Osiris, in funeral ceremonies, and was originally the sole bearer of the most distinctive item of priestly dress, the panther-skin. Other priestly insignia are rare, although the high priest of Ptah wore a complicated necklace with the shape of an elongated jackal. In later periods priests were distinguished by their shaven heads and often in cult wore a panther-skin. Beside the *se(te)m* the principal officiants at rituals were the *imy-khent*, 'man in the fore', acting rather as a palace master of ceremonies, and above all the 'bearer of the ritual text' or lector-priest who would hold up the papyrus and roll it forward as the ceremonies proceeded to ensure that they conformed to written tradition. Lector-priests could be divided into the 'ordinary' and the 'master', and master lector-priests constitute in later texts the entourage of Pharaoh, as depicted in the Biblical story of the Exodus. Beside the usual cursive script for administration, literary texts and letters, a lector-priest needed to know the full hieroglyphic forms of the signs, in which the ritual texts were written, and indeed 'lector-priest' could be paraphrased in later texts both by the term 'scribe of the house of life' and, in Greek translation, *hierogrammateus*, 'one who wrote in the sacred script'. Just as the house of life formed the institution for transmitting knowledge and so maintaining the Pharaonic world view, so we meet in the lector-priest the person who spent his life preserving and producing the hieroglyphic core of that tradition.

57 Stela of Sarenenutet, entitled 'the revered one who gives divine offerings to the gods, accountant of the double (i.e. national) granary, steward'. The formula stipulates as always that the *ka* (soul of sustenance) of the man be granted a share in the food offerings from the king to the gods. 12th Dynasty, *c.* 1950 BC; limestone, from Abydos. H. 52 cm. EA 585.

4

SURVIVING LIFE

Protection of the Body

THE COSMIC ENVIRONMENT INSTALLED BY RA and the mythic cycle of Osiris and Horus created the framework of space and time for human existence. This framework was sustained by the cult and festivals perpetuated in temples throughout Egypt. Outside the temple walls life carried on as precariously as it was perceived within them. Until very recently humanity knew few sure defences against the battery of diseases that may assail any person at any moment from birth to old age – if they are lucky enough to reach it. Treatment of internal ailments remained particularly ill-founded in the ignorance of the inner workings of the human body, and even for the better-understood external causes of suffering such as wounds from tools or weapons the remedies did not include effective control of pain. The Egyptians responded to these problems with what we tend to divide prejudicially into prayer, 'primitive' medicine and 'magic', but which in the sources themselves build up a unitary approach to the world.

In the first place the Egyptians recognised the human being as a combination of physical and non-physical elements, each of which might be approached separately and each of which required nurturing. A Late Period funerary text included in the 'incantations for going out in the necropolis by day' (the *Book of the Dead*) demonstrates the lengths to which the Egyptians subdivided the human being into independently discernible parts:

> *O you who fetch* ba-*spirits, O you who fell shades,*
> *O all deities within, at the head of the living,*
> *come, bring the* ba-*spirit of (the deceased);*
> *may his heart be sweet, may it join his body,*
> *his* ba-*spirit to his body, to his heart;*
> *may his* ba-*spirit embrace his body and his heart;*
> *may they fetch him, the gods in the shrine of the primeval stone*
> *in Iunu beside Shu son of Atum,*
> *his heart like that of Ra, his heart like that of Khepri;*
> *twice purification to his* ka-*spirit, to his* ba-*spirit, to his*
> *corpse, to his shade, to his mummy;*
> *he shall never perish before the lord of the sacred land (the necropolis).*

In addition to the body and its heart, seat of life, the person is endowed with a shadow and with two spirits, one named *ba* and the other *ka*. The shadow recalls the modern European notion of the 'shade' as part of the surviving nature of a human being. The *ka* is a part of human nature in hieroglyphic texts from the Old Kingdom to the Roman Period, and is a word that coincides with words for 'bull' and 'food'. The link with 'bull' would imply both potency and the passage of male seed at conception, tying the individual to the generations that preceded him in his family line. The connection with 'food' is explicit in the innumerable texts for offerings for the dead, made according to the Egyptian formula 'for the *ka* of' a specific person. The *ba* appears in the Old Kingdom as embodiment of the power of king and gods to make their presence manifest in the world, and is often cited in the plural as *bau* of a deity or of a place, the sum of its divine beings; *bau* of Nekhen and Buto thus represent the numinous protective power at the southern and northern ends of Egypt, and were shown respectively as jackal- and falcon-headed trios, three for the plural and nine for totality. From the Middle Kingdom on, each individual human being was also said to have one *ba*-spirit, as the funerary cult for mortals adopted the format for that of the king. The *ba* expressed above all the ability to move, portrayed in two- and three-dimensional representation as a bird or human-headed bird, the head to identify the being as a human spirit, the body to illustrate the attribute of mobility, nothing else being as free and mobile as a bird of flight.

58 Scene from the *Book of the Dead* of Hunefer in which he appears with his *ba* (soul of mobility) shown separately behind him; both are in adoration of the sun-god as a disk on the mountain of the horizon between the lions of yesterday and today. 19th Dynasty, *c*. 1285 BC; painted papyrus, from Thebes. H. 39.5 cm. EA 9901, part.

59 Segment from a hollow cuboid rod with representations of forces that might ward off danger at childbirth; on this segment a turtle appears between two frogs. Originally a small figure of a turtle would have been attached to one of the undecorated sides. Late Middle Kingdom, $c.$1750 BC; steatite, of unknown provenance. L 5.2 cm. EA 22892.

The birth of any individual brings a day of joy, but also of peril, especially acute in a world without antibiotics. Various divine beings came to the assistance of the pregnant mother before or at childbirth, in some cases taking monstrous forms that would frighten away any harmful forces. The frog Heqet was an image of plenty, as was the serpent-goddess of harvest and abundance Renenutet, 'the nurturer'; the birth-brick upon which the mother crouched to let the child emerge as painlessly as possible was called *meskhenet* and could also be personified as a female deity. A male deity often shown in New Kingdom and later depictions of birth and rebirth is Shay, 'destiny', incorporation of all that has been appointed to a person, the framework of time and space into which they have been born. A New Kingdom tale of a predestined prince sets the scene with the arrival of seven Hathor goddesses at the birth to warn that the prince was destined to die by dog, snake or crocodile. The notion that a person had an allotted timespan often occurs in texts, but there was also the possibility that other divine forces may conspire either to shorten or to lengthen that time; thus a person is always in a position to pray for a long life as well as a good burial. The god Khnum played his role at birth as the fashioner of the material being of humans, as a potter uses clay to fashion pots. Whereas these deities had for the most part regular features in Egyptian iconography, the frog Heqet stands somewhat outside the usual stock of nature used to represent divinity; the same is true of the leonine dwarf Bes and the goddess of childbirth depicted as a pregnant hippopotamus.

Although the least regular in depiction, the two last were perhaps the most familiar of these childbirth deities. The hippopotamus goddess is identified variously as Ipet, Taweret, 'the great goddess' and Rerct, 'the sow'; the last of these names suggests that the goddess was perceived in part as having the character of the sow that tends its children but is also capable of devouring them, a dramatic union of life to be nurtured and most horrific death to be averted. Although the hippopotamus also provided an appropriate representation of power as a river animal liable to obstruct and even destroy light craft, the pig seems to constitute part of the underlying imagery; it was presumably named but not depicted because it contravened the rules of religious propriety, for pigs were omnivorous and therefore broke the bounds not only of cleanliness, by living on waste, but also of classification, by not living like the other scavengers – cats and dogs – on meat alone.

Early representations of the dwarflike deity suggest a lion seen from the front, contrary to the usual rules of representation in which the profile of the head was

60 ABOVE Headrest of the royal scribe Qenherkhepshef with the image of Bes spitting and wielding serpents and holding a spear in defence of the vulnerable sleeper, in this case perhaps the deceased. 19th Dynasty, $c.$ 1225 BC; limestone, from Deir el-Medina, Thebes. H. 18 cm. EA 63783.

61 LEFT Figure of Bes, perhaps from an item of furniture. New Kingdom, $c.$ 1350 BC (?); ivory, from Thebes (?). H. 6.5 cm. EA 17072.

62 OPPOSITE Figure of the goddess for protecting mother and child, in the form of a pregnant hippopotamus with crocodile-back. Here the goddess wears the horned sun-disk and double plume headdress. Late Period, after 600 BC (?); blue glazed composition, of unknown provenance. H. 20 cm. EA 13162.

taken as its most easily recognisable aspect. In a limestone relief of $c.$ 2400 BC a male figure in a register labelled 'dancing by children' is shown with a leonine head and carrying a staff which has a human hand at the tip; this is an early example of the association of the leonine head with childhood. In the Middle Kingdom the leonine dwarf reappears with the label Aha, 'the fighting deity', on flat curving ivory 'wands' carved from hippopotamus tusks and used as markers on the ground, perhaps in a circle around the bed of pregnant mother or baby child. Other defending powers are shown on such markers, including the pregnant hippopotamus and such figures as the winged griffin. On a headrest of somewhat later date the leonine dwarf, a rising griffin and the pregnant hippopotamus wield knives to protect the defenceless sleeper. Later periods name the leonine dwarf-god and a female counterpart as Bes and Beset.

63 Ointment container in the form of a woman holding a horn-shaped ointment vessel and with her child strapped to her back. It is thought that the oils in such vessels were used at childbirth. 18th Dynasty, c.1400 BC; painted terracotta, of unknown provenance. H. 12.2 cm. EA 24652.

Modern commentators often classify such deities of childbirth as 'popular' in supposed opposition to the deities promoted in the temples by the state cult. The distinction is arbitrary, as shown not only by the inclusion of childbirth deities in temple decoration, and in the case of Ipet at Thebes as the proprietor of a temple, but more obviously by the presence of the same deities at royal as at non-royal births. The sadly vandalised paintings of the Theban palace of Amenhotep III at Malqata included earlier this century depictions of Bes standing and dancing. A similar false division has been applied to texts to fend off death at and after birth; Egyptologists tend to call the texts that they accept as 'scientific "medical" texts', and the texts that they reject as 'superstitious "magical" texts', an approach nowhere more clearly fallible than in the labelling of one papyrus in the British Museum as the London Medical Papyrus and another of similar content as the Harris Magical Papyrus. The ancient manuscripts themselves divided the sphere of caring for the sick and endangered in a more pragmatic manner; they grouped together the prognoses, diagnoses and prescribed treatments under the term *shesau*, and often compiled separately the lists of ingredients for medicaments and recipes for their preparation under the term *pekheret*, 'prescription'. A third, and in Egyptian eyes no less important, part of any act of healing consisted of the words to be spoken while the treatment was carried out or the medicament applied; these formulaic recitals were called *ru*, 'incantations', a term that covered also the texts recited in temple rituals and festivals, as well as funerary texts for a good afterlife.

The three types of text, *shesau*, *pekheret* and *ru*, belong together in any one action of doctor for patient, and cannot be separated into fully independent categories of 'medical' and 'magical' according to modern tastes. Some texts apply the heading *meket hau*, 'protection of the body', that could well serve as the label for all these 'medical-magical' records: it captures the kernel of everything the Egyptians were endeavouring to achieve in these objects and images, in writing and in representation. Others take a term from ritual originally intended for the defence of the king, the 'selection of the back', in other words the guarding of the most vulnerable part of the body. The same phrase was already extended to the royal palace in the Old Kingdom. In the various texts for the protection of the body the mingling of what we find acceptable with what we do not runs through each of the three types, prescriptions, treatments and incantations. The ingredients of the medicaments range from plants with what would still today be recognised as healing properties to ingredients of symbolic force. Prognoses cover what we call the irrational as well as forecasts moulded by practical experience; thus the likely physical consequences of certain snakebites were observed with harsh accuracy, while equally a healer might predict from the breath of a woman who had slept on an onion bulb whether she was pregnant or not. The incantations, most uniformly rejected by Egyptologists as 'non-medical', merely present a more tightly structured expression of the rule that healing cannot be confined to physical treatment but must extend to social communication as well, a principle that is receiving wider recognition again today.

Treatment in life began at childbirth, a time that claimed most lives, as much of mothers as of children. If the child did not die it was given a most important part of its being, its name; Egyptian texts treat the name as part of the person on a par with the body, heart, shadow, *ka* and *ba*. Destruction of the name brought annihilation, denying a person eternal life and reducing him or her to a state of perpetual death. One of the penalties for high treason was loss of name, and the conspirators against Ramses III had their names changed from blessings such as Ramose, 'Ra is the one who gave birth to me', to Ramesdsu, 'Ra is the one who hates him', or Bakenamun, 'servant of Amun', to Pabakkamen 'the blind servant'; This reversed the original intention of the name, to give thanks for the child and to secure for it a good life. In the early first millennium BC the effort to protect the child expanded to requesting from deities their protection for life, with every possible threat specified in a series of clauses like a general insurance policy. The deity would issue the decree detailing this protection at an oracle, in the role of 'the great and mighty god who first took form', and the text was copied onto papyrus, rolled up and placed in a tube to be worn on a string around the neck. The practice was no more confined to a 'folk' level than were the ivory markers of the Middle Kingdom; one was made out for the son of a king Osorkon, and included the prospect that the child would grow to lead the army of Pharaoh on campaigns and return with glad tidings. The following extracts from the words of the deities issuing the decree for a girl called Buir-harkhons exemplify the detail of these documents; they reveal many sources of danger felt by the Egyptians in their world and not otherwise voiced in the surviving record.

> *We will save her from Sekhmet and her son;*
> *we will save her from the fall of a wall, from the crash of thunder . . .*
> *we will save her from every death, from every disease . . .*
> *from every evil eye, from every evil glare . . .*
> *we will save her from the gods who seize people by stealth, from the gods who find people in the countryside and kill them in the town or vice versa;*
> *we will save her from every god and every goddess who take aspects of power when they are not pacified;*
> *we will save her from the gods who seize people in place of others.*

These among other clauses were vouchsafed by two forms of Khons; the document closes with words of another Theban deity, Mont in the form Mont-Ra-Horakhty, with his consort Iunyt, 'the goddess of Armant', whose clauses include the following:

We will save her from a Great Power at a canal, from a Great Power at a well, from a Great Power at a river-branch, from a Great Power at a lake, from a Great Power at a pool left by the flood, from a male Great Power, from a female Great Power, from a Great Power of her father or of her mother, from a Great Power of the family of her father or of the family of her mother;
we will appease them for her, we will make her safe and sound from them on her every day of life;
we will save her from the power of a Syrian, from the power of a Nubian, from the power of a western nomad, from the power of an Egyptian, from the power of a man of power, from the power of a woman of power, from any power of any ilk.

64 Curved staff to brandish against enemies of the mother and child, adorned with images of defending forces including, at centre, the scarab beetle of rebirth, to its left, a full frontal figure with leonine head, and to the right end the snarling pregnant hippopotamus with crocodile-back. The staff was broken in antiquity, perhaps when it was placed in a burial. Its presence in a burial for protection at (re-)birth would be desired but it may have been thought too powerful to be kept in one piece next to the dead. Late Middle Kingdom, $c.$1750 BC; ivory, from Thebes. L. 37 cm. EA 18175.

In these last clauses the word for power is *heka*, the same term found in chapter one to denote the creative power of the sun-god emerging out of nothingness. It could be used to refer to texts written or spoken to achieve ends beyond the reach of normal word and action, and is often translated as 'magic', and 'man of power' as 'magician'. Those terms are avoided here because they arouse a modern European prejudice that marginalises what we call 'magic' to forbidden margins of society, whereas the creative word in Egypt is neutral in itself, open to good and bad use. The employment of *heka* the creative word reaches the heart of cult and cosmos in the service of king and sun-god maintaining the world; the image of the cobra on the forehead of the ruler could be named Werethekau, 'the goddess great in *heka*-power', and hymns to the royal insignia address this defensive power to fight back as much as any one crown or diadem.

The power named *heka* could be used in the positive role of defending human beings against illness but could also be put into effect by evildoers or those who wished to harm the individual, such as the Egyptian and foreign 'men of *heka*-

power' cited in the text above. Foreign languages were regarded as particularly potent at certain periods, presumably because the difficulty in understanding them made them appear more able to harbour hidden powers and effects. In the time of Tutankhamun, when substantial contact with other Near Eastern lands had become long established, the compilers of the so-called London Medical Papyrus included as defence against disease a number of incantations in Syrian-Palestinian and in Aegean languages. The late second millennium also witnessed the entry of a number of Syrian deities into Egyptian iconography, such as Anat and Astarte as companions of the royal chariot into battle, and Qedeshet and Reshep as defenders from storm and ailment. Another Syrian-Palestinian deity Hurun was identified with an Egyptian term *huru* applied to the Great Sphinx at Giza, and became part of the reinterpretation of that monument as a manifestation of the sun-god as Horus-in-the-horizon.

The incantations for defence against disease match the list of perils enunciated in the amuletic decrees of the early first millennium BC. From *c.*1750 BC surviving examples on papyrus take the model of deities, above all Isis and the child Horus in the marshes, but also other gods, including even the sun-god himself; a text of defence known on Ramesside papyri recounts in full the tale of how Ra, bitten by a snake, was in such agony that he revealed his name, and thus his identity and power, to Isis in return for her promise to heal him. In the late second millennium BC the image of the child Horus as Shed, 'the saviour', was depicted in control of noxious creatures on wooden stelae. In the Late Period the Horus stelae became more elaborate with extensive texts, in part built on Ramesside antecedents and in part developing new themes such as the tale of Isis and the seven scorpions cited in chapter two. The later Horus stelae are generally of dark stone, sometimes steatite but sometimes of more costly material, such as that of king Nakhthorheb in basalt, and are distinguished particularly by having a representation of Horus no longer in two dimensions as in the earlier wooden stelae but in the round. In the middle of the history of transmission of these texts stands a remarkable group statue of Ramses III inscribed with some of the same texts that occur on the Horus stela of Nakhthorheb eight centuries later; it was set on the road east of Iunu (Heliopolis) to ward off the evils of the desert from the approaches to the city of the sun-god.

Some of the texts open with the full identification of the sufferer or the healer with the deity, as in the tale with the seven scorpions where the first words 'I am Isis' are confirmed at its close, 'May the child live and the poison die, then shall Horus be healthy for his mother Isis', to which one of the three copies adds 'and then shall the patient be healthy for his mother likewise'. One of the copies of this tale is preserved on a unique Late Period papyrus which bears beside the text a vivid outline drawing of men on boats with a catch of wildfowl, others on land with the birdtrap and a third group of men collecting papyrus. This combination of countryside scenes and text for defence against scorpion bites indicates the stark contrast between the idyllic settings with which we are familiar from tomb-chapel reliefs and paintings and the unsettling imagery and language of the texts for the protection of the body; both worlds are one and the same, and the Egyptian living in the midst of such dangers would have felt acute need for defence.

65 Front and back of a plaque showing Horus. On one side he is depicted as Shed, 'the saviour', with power over dangerous animals, here serpents, gazelle, lion and crocodiles. The other side shows him as a falcon with the Double Crown and flail of kingship and with three snakes emerging from the ground at his feet. New Kingdom, c. 1250 BC (?); wood, of unknown provenance. H. 5.3 cm. EA 65842. Drawn by Christine Barratt.

The sharpness of the danger produced a keen observation of the smaller risks to life, scorpions and snakes; the only surviving Pharaonic text with a classification scheme approaching the standards of modern zoologists and botanists is a compendium detailing every species of serpent, their external appearance, their capacity to bite or not, and the effects of and chances of survival from their bites. A typical entry from the first part of the papyrus detailing thirty-eight species runs as follows:

As for the cobra serpent, with the hue of sand, if it bites a man he suffers on the side that was not pierced and does not suffer on the side with the bite; it is an illness that I can treat. Carry out for him everything with many emetics and bleedings [?] after he vomits. It operates for Seth. The person bitten by it shall not die.

The last entry in the section gives a remarkable account of the chameleon, a harmless reptile that nonetheless provokes suspicion in many cultures because of its ability to camouflage itself:

As for the chameleon, it is entirely green but for a white stomach, having two underlegs and on its back three divisions, two to the fore and the other to the rear. If it fastens onto things it takes their hue. One can be protected for it up to seven days. It operates as Anubis. They (?) can be exorcised by appeasing it.

The listing of species is followed by the 'compendium of treatments for people, to remove the poison of any snake male or female, of any scorpion, of any worm, in the hands of the exorciser of Serqet, as well as warding off any reptiles and sealing their mouths'. The naming of the exorciser of Serqet as the title for men treating poisonous bites seems specific, but other sources appear to allow for considerable overlap between different titles of healing professionals. The compendium of prescriptions now known as Papyrus Ebers, after its nineteenth-century owner, is a book of incantations to be recited when applying the medicaments; it is said to be for 'any physician, any priest of Sekhmet, any protector' involved in physical treatment. It is not yet possible to determine the exact activity implied in each of these designations and that of exorciser of Serqet.

The cobra did not kill, as the above entry observes, but it was among the most common of harmful snakes in Egypt and perhaps for this reason provided the image of the *iaret*, 'rising serpent', or uraeus, on the brow of the king, the goddess of the Theban necropolis Merseger, 'lover of silence', and the goddess of harvest fields Renenutet, 'nurturer'. The royal tomb workmen at Deir el-Medina set two-dimensional images of serpents at their doorways, and contemporary inhabitants of lower or middle class houses at Memphis fashioned cobras of clay with miniature offering bowls; in both instances the enemy became the guardian of the home. The practice found new form in the Ptolemaic Period when the male and female serpent were identified as Osiris and Isis, as the *agathodaimon*, 'good spirit', watching over human well-being. As an inhabitant of the earth the snake could also represent the first deity as the primeval snake, in such images as the uroboros, or snake

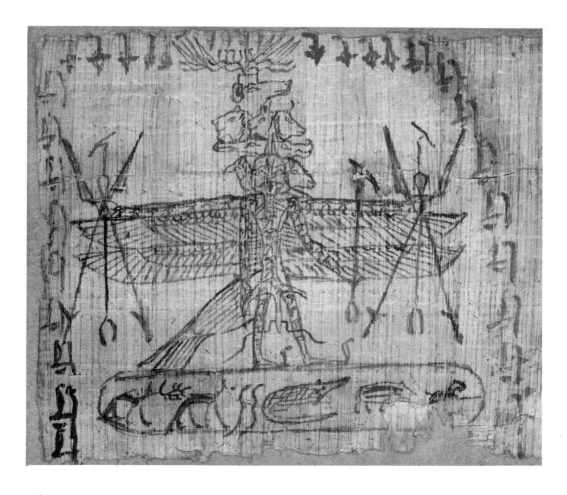

66, 67 and 68 Three images of the creator god as the totality of all powerful and potentially dangerous forces of the universe. The core figure is that of Bes, identified in the Late Period as the force at not only each human birth but also at the source of life itself; upon this core is built a composite union of attributes. ABOVE The figurine presents the dwarflike body of Bes with baboon head, wings and sun-disk, while the papyrus (OPPOSITE) adds a lion, canines and ram to the head and serpents to the feet. At the bottom of the papyrus appears a row of dangerous animals, similar to that on an actual figurine where the groundline consists of a serpent eating its own tail, a symbol of eternity (BELOW).

FIGURINE Late Period, after 600 BC; green glazed composition, of unknown provenance. H. 5.2 cm. EA 11900.

PAPYRUS Late Period, 4th century BC or later; papyrus, of unknown provenance. H. 9.2 cm. EA 10296.

ROW OF ANIMALS Late Period, after 600 BC; green glazed composition, of unknown provenance. H. 5.3 cm. EA 11989. Drawn by Christine Barratt.

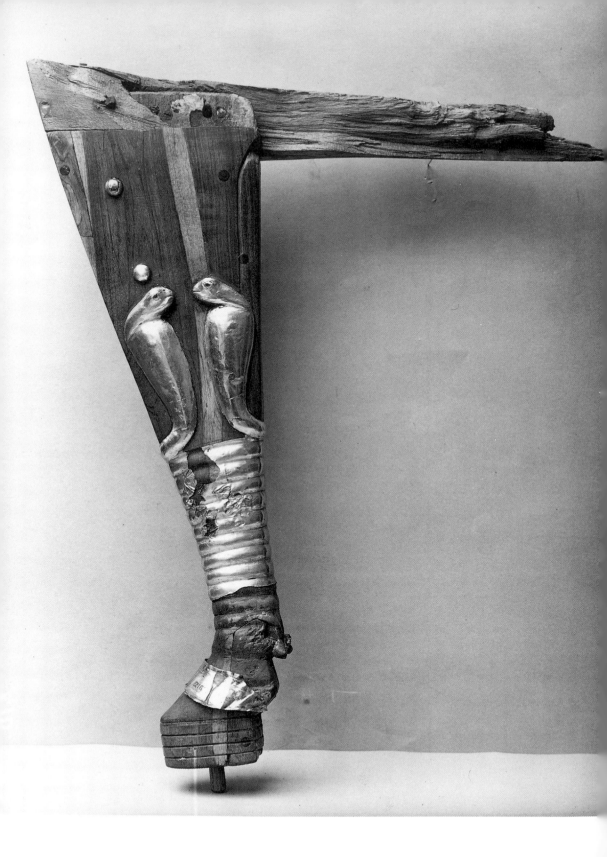

69 ABOVE Cobra from a household shrine, designed to protect the family just as the uraeus protected the brow of the king. New Kingdom, $c.$ 1325 BC; painted clay, from Amarna. H. 13 cm. EA 55594.

70 OPPOSITE Fragment from a bed with figures of cobras entwined around the leg as symbols of protection. New Kingdom, $c.$ 1450 BC (?); wood with gold sheet ornament, from Thebes. H. 46.1 cm. EA 21574.

swallowing its own tail, symbolising eternity and shown around the newborn sun-god.

Scorpions won the same respect and the kingship festival included in the earliest records a scorpion-goddess at the side of the king. She was perhaps identical to the later deity named Serqet, 'she who allows to breathe' – so-called because a scorpion bite causes a person to stop breathing remarkably rapidly and so the scorpion had the power of life and death, breathing or not breathing, over mortals. One title for healers was that of 'exorciser of Serqet', a position enumerated among the staff of expeditions sent to the eastern deserts to procure stone, an area where the hazard of scorpion bite loomed even larger than within the valley. Another designation of healers was 'pure-priest of Sekhmet' and incantations against plague in particular invoke that goddess, as on the fragment of a writing board now in the British Museum:

[he will not] depart (life) on his bed, he will not die on [z. . . . . . if] this incantation is spoken over an image of Sekhmet [. . . . . .] in a year of plague, it is an amulet [. . .].

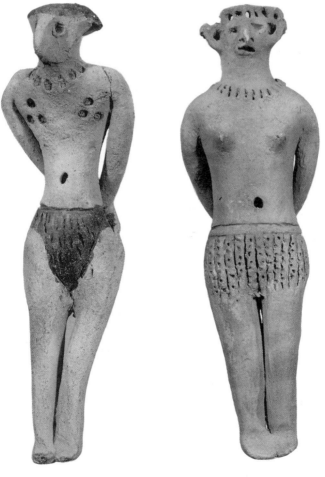

71 Curse figures representing enemies to be destroyed in rites of defending the realm. Similar figures have been found covered with the names and titles of the enemies to be annihilated; loss of name and title amounted to total destruction in Egyptian eyes. Middle Kingdom, *c.* 1900 BC (?); painted terracotta, of unknown provenance. H. of left figure 13 cm.
EA 56928, 56912–4.

Plague struck the rich as the poor, as throughout Europe during the Black Death or in London in 1665. A letter from the unique archive of diplomatic correspondence found at the Residence of Akhenaten reveals that an image of Ishtar was sent from Babylon to aid Amenhotep III, and a Ptolemaic stela preserves a tradition that Ramses II sent an image from Thebes to cure a Near Eastern monarch. Texts for the protection of the body sometimes include assertions that they were shown to work in particular reigns, such as examples in the London Medical Papyrus said to have been efficacious in the time of Amenhotep III against the 'Asiatic' pestilence.

Fear of harmful animals was matched by fear of death on water, naturally enough in a country where the Nile provided the principal means of transportation and where death on the river would have taken the toll of human life that land highways exact today. The manuscript now known as the Harris Magical Papyrus is more precisely a collection of hymns to the primeval deities followed by incantations to avert disaster on the Nile, expressed in Egyptian as 'all books (literally papyrus-rolls) to be chanted on water'. In one the reciter takes the role of

the first son of the sun-god Shu and is thus able to intimidate the threatening crocodile – a reminder that perhaps even more than drowning, the Egyptian dreaded the fate of being capsized and then snatched to a slower and more cruel death. One literary tale copied *c.* 1600 B C pictures a wise man using his knowledge of *heka*-power to take revenge on his wife and her lover by fashioning a model crocodile and casting it into the water to come to life and attack his enemies. It may be remarked here that the surviving record includes extremely few such uses of *heka*-power, that is of texts to be chanted, for destructive ends, possibly because destructive power was too dangerous to record on papyrus and commit to the sources from which we derive our knowledge of ancient Egypt. An example of destructive power which does survive is that of the state against political enemies. At all periods figurines were made of bound captives and these or pottery vessels could be inscribed with the names of all the enemies of the king of Egypt at home and, in greatest detail, abroad, and then smashed and buried. At the Middle Kingdom fortress of Mirgissa in Nubia a horde of such 'curse texts' was found in the desert, marking a reinforcement of the military defences with the power of word and image.

As part of the armoury against premature death Egyptians wore amulets showing the healing eye of the creator or of Horus, or images of deities such as Sekhmet herself. These amulets were once thought to be primarily funerary in use, but now, thanks to more careful excavation and recording of finds, they have been found in settlement sites, as in the early first-millennium B C houses at Khemenu (Hermopolis to the Greeks; modern Ashmunein) in Middle Egypt. Amulets in the shape of deities or divine symbols were placed on the bodies of the dead from the Old Kingdom to the Roman Period, and they may have been worn in life throughout the same time range. From the earliest to the latest periods there is also evidence of votive objects, items that were placed in temples or chapels as prayers in concrete form, to offer thanks or to plead for help. In the first millennium B C these became particularly common as small faience or bronze figures, mass-produced with the casting techniques then available; the late periods also witnessed a growth in demand for the interpretation of dreams, sometimes involving paying a priest to sleep at a sanctuary and reveal his dream and its interpretation to the client. The Egyptians saw in the dream a 'revelation of truth', as it is put in the Middle Kingdom composition the *Instruction of king Amenemhat* I, where the old king appears to his son to warn him of the perils of assassins. The only surviving dream-book from the Pharaonic Period is a Ramesside copy, but the language of the text suggests an earlier date of composition, perhaps even in the Middle Kingdom. The entries reveal the fears and expectations of an Egyptian of the second millennium B C, as the examples below may indicate.

> *If a man see himself in a dream slaying a hippopotamus: good, a large meal from the Palace.*
> *If a man sees himself in a dream plunging into the river: good, it means purification from all evil.*
> *If a man sees himself in a dream making love to a woman: bad, it means mourning.*

If a man sees himself in a dream looking at an ostrich: bad, *harm will befall him.*
If a man sees himself in a dream feeding cattle: bad, *it means wandering the earth.*
If a man sees himself in a dream casting wood into water: bad, *bringing suffering to his house.*

The same fragmentary papyrus goes on to specify a different type of man, modelled not on the orderly Horus but on the disorderly Seth and exemplified by the drunkard. A different set of dreams with interpretations followed for these 'followers of Seth', but it is impossible in the absence of parallels to know how many deities were involved in this classification of human beings. It seems most likely that only Horus and Seth provided models for the classification, but we cannot tell whether this division of mankind into orderly and disorderly (rather than good and evil) was a perception shared widely throughout the country and at different times. Only its existence as the Ramesside Theban copy of perhaps a Middle Kingdom text would indicate a more general belief in the approach than the survival of a single source might suggest.

Somewhat better attested are the calendars of lucky and unlucky days, in which each day or even each third part of each day received the note 'good' or 'bad'. The more elaborate texts record the reasons for classifying dates as good or bad, taking events in the world of the gods as good or ill omen. The earliest calendar of lucky and unlucky days presents each day regardless of month with a single note and without reasons given; it dates to *c.* 1800 B C and was found in the Middle Kingdom town near modern Lahun at the mouth of the Fayum. Two ostraca (flakes of limestone used as writing surfaces) and six papyri of the Ramesside Period or its immediate aftermath continued the tradition of which two examples contain the most extended commentaries on the mythical prototypes. An entry on one of the two more expansive commentaries gives the following reason why a good morning and midday should turn to an ill-omened evening:

First month of inundation, day 25: good, good, bad: do not go out on this day in the evening; on this day Sekhmet went out to the eastern mountain against the confederacy of Seth.

The various manuscripts do not always agree on the character of a day, but the five days added to the end of each year of 360 days (twelve months of thirty days each) were universally regarded as a time of danger. The records of work on the royal tomb at Thebes in the thirteenth and twelfth centuries B C also conform to the recommendations of the calendars only on the five days at the end of the year, when activity in the Valley of the Kings ceased. Differences between the calendars are not easy to explain, but may have arisen either from variations in local tradition or from the compilation of separate horoscopes for individuals. Egypt provides little supporting evidence for the practices common in Mesopotamia of inspecting animal entrails as a guide to the future, or for the Roman practice of auguring from birds; the zodiac too appears in Egypt only in the later periods as an import from Babylon, whereas in Pharaonic times the star-charts on coffin lids and the ceilings of burial chambers were intended to show the deceased the time of night or day rather than the course of events to come.

Most of the techniques above aim at the defensive goal of surviving life; few texts of the Pharaonic Period reflect personal efforts to destroy enemies, or on the positive side to secure the love of another. References to the 'evil eye', as in the amuletic decrees cited above, envisage such effects as in the hands of others, and may spring from a widespread fear of evil action rather than actual usage by evil-minded people. A rare record of evil practice occurs among the trials of the men and women accused of plotting the death of Ramses III; in their conspiracy they were alleged to have made wax figures of the palace guards as part of the physical measures to overpower them. Such occult methods may have been deemed necessary to break through the defensive shield of energy around the dwelling of

72, 73 and 74 Five representations of female fertility to be placed in the grave as a guarantee of eternal rebirth. Such figures are often erroneously called dolls, but clearly emphasise the pubic triangle and in some cases reduce the human female figure to a headless and limbless torso. They are not concubines of the dead either; funerary texts do exist to provide evidence of the belief in sexual intercourse in the next world but female fertility figures could be placed in burials of women as well as men. The headgear of the bronze figure (OPPOSITE LEFT) may allude to the role of the god's wife of Amun as the female element in the life-giving power of the god and is typical of the period after the New Kingdom. ABOVE Late Middle Kingdom, c.1750 BC; painted wood with clay faces and hair. H. of centre figure 23 cm. EA 22612, 22631, 22632. OPPOSITE LEFT Third Intermediate Period, c.850 BC; bronze, of unknown provenance. H. 23 cm. EA 55019. OPPOSITE RIGHT Late Middle Kingdom, c.1750 BC; clay, from Thebes. H. 19.2 cm. EA 49152.

the king, although it is also possible that this part of the conspiracy was imagined by the accusers, much as the accusers of witches in European tradition once evolved lurid details in their accounts of what the accused were alleged to have done. In either case the trial documents establish that such methods were thought available to evildoers; an actual wax figurine enclosing a piece of hair in the collections of the British Museum attests to use in real life, but may date to the Roman Period or later. The text in which a man uses a wax crocodile to attack his personal enemies (cited above) is part of literary tale, and again does not necessarily establish the existence of such techniques, rather than just the fear of them, in ancient life.

Objects and texts that are sometimes now described as love-charms tend rather to be preoccupied with childbirth, as might be expected in a land where children were considered so important for the individual. Figures of women reduced in many cases to exaggerated portrayals of female genitalia have in the past been seen as 'concubines of the dead', to allow a dead person to enjoy sexual intercourse in the next life and have been identified as dolls in many studies. Although their sexual role can scarcely be in doubt and finds a corollary in funerary texts to maintain sexual power after death, the Egyptians did not draw such a clear distinction between enjoyment of sexual intercourse and need of procreation. The goddess who answered the Egyptian aspirations in the entire area that we subdivide into love, marriage and motherhood was Hathor. She was portrayed as a woman in her aspect of sexual partner, and as a cow in her aspect of tender mother, reflecting the Egyptian observation of cow and calf in nature, by which the word *ames*, 'to show concern for another', was written in hieroglyphs with the end-sign of a cow turning her head to lick her suckling calf. At shrines of Hathor on the West Bank of Thebes at Deir el-Bahri and in Nubia at Faras supplicants left figures of a woman or a phallus as three-dimensional prayers to the goddess for a child. The king also placed himself under the tutelage of Hathor, and her name indicates an original royal role as the 'house of Horus', either as the wife or the mother of the god. The shrine at Deir el-Bahri was either founded under Hatshepsut or more likely then became a focus of royal and thus national cult, and Thutmose III and his son Amenhotep II installed in the cliff sanctuary a statue of the goddess as a cow with the king as her son taking milk from her udder. Until the Late Period Hathor was the only goddess to possess temples of her own throughout the country, with a major sanctuary as the goddess of the southern sycamore at Memphis. As goddess of sensuality she also covered the sphere of music, especially in temple ritual where the sistrum, a metal rattle, accompanied the cult. Her cult centre in Upper Egypt at Dendera became a principal recipient of royal largesse in the Ptolemaic Period and in its late form is today one of the best-preserved of Egyptian temples.

The survival of life and the goal of self-fulfilment did not take effect solely on the supernatural plane as a struggle among unseen forces of good and evil. Egyptian texts are among the first surviving written testimonies to the human need for society, to a 'need to be recognised', as the German author Christa Wolf has phrased it. Already in the Old Kingdom the owner of a tomb-chapel felt constrained to assert his moral right to the monument that assured his afterlife; the claim that the tomb had been built on new ground, that the builders had been recompensed for their labours and that the stone had not been taken from older monuments amounted to a self-justification that gave the owner the right to sue any damager of his own monument in the tribunal of the afterlife, or even to attack them directly in this world. The inscriptions of a court official Meni, who lived probably in the Sixth Dynasty, include the following two texts, on blocks from his tomb-chapel:

> *As to any man, I have done this without ever harming him;*
> *as to my craftsman in my burial place, I have satisfied him.*
> *The elder of the portal Meni declares:*
> *the crocodile on him in the water,*
> *the snake on him on land,*
> *on the man who will do things against this, though nothing has ever been done against him.*
> *It is the god who will judge him.*

By the end of the third millennium B C such texts had grown into longer catalogues of virtues that reveal to us a common humanity, as exemplified in the inscription from the tomb-chapel of a man named Neferseshemra, or Sheshi for short:

> *I have gone out from my city, I have come down from my district,*
> *I have done Right for myself for her lord,*
> *I have satisfied him with what he always loves;*
> *I have spoken Right, I have done Right,*
> *I have spoken well, I have done well,*
> *I have seized the good moment.*
> *Love of me is good there among people.*
> *I judged two brothers so they were (both) content;*
> *I rescued the wretch from the man mightier than him when I had authority in the case.*
> *I gave bread to the hungry, clothing (to the naked),*
> *a crossing to the boatless, a burial to the man without a son.*
> *I acted as ferryboat to the man without a ferry.*
> *I respected my father, was gracious to my mother;*
> *I nurtured their children.*

From *c.* 1800 B C to the Roman Period an entire genre of texts known as *sebayt*, 'instructions', and written primarily in the cursive scripts on papyrus, presented the knowledge of experience that might allow a man success in life; although until the latest periods these are oriented to the élite literate stratum of society, and although they exclude women from start to finish, the instructions give a detailed portrayal of the ways in which the Egyptians expected to succeed in their very social life on this earth. The instructions found a brilliant parallel in a second literary genre, the lament, in which the correct rules of behaviour and the correct order are minutely delineated by the description of their absence, a world in which all the norms of good have been overturned and chaos stalks the land. Modern scholars have tended to see in these laments a literal account of historical distress, specifically the collapse of the unified state at the end of the third millennium B C before its

75 and 76 Hathor represented as a cow on (ABOVE) the funerary garment for a child from Deir el-Bahri and (OPPOSITE) the stela of Khabekhenet, a craftsman of the royal tomb. On the garment, the Theban cliffside can be discerned to the left of the cow while in the stela it engulfs all but the cow's head, shoulders and front legs. GARMENT 18th Dynasty, c.1350 BC (?); painted linen, from Deir el-Bahri, Thebes. H. 34.3 cm. EA 43071. STELA 19th Dynasty, c.1200 BC; limestone, from Deir el-Medina, Thebes. H. 63 cm. EA 555.

77 and 78 The sistrum, along with the human voice, provided the main musical accompaniment to cult rituals, an aspect appropriate to Hathor in her role as goddess of sensuality. Accordingly it is often decorated with the Hathor face of a woman with the ears of a cow and typical heavy curling wig. The example here (LEFT) adds figures of cats, suggesting that it was used in the cult of Bast. Another evocation of the sensuous was the *menit* (OPPOSITE), or 'counterpoise' to heavy necklaces. These too were often decorated with the Hathor face and could be made as separate votive objects, as were both examples here. SISTRUM Late Period, after 600 BC; bronze, of unknown provenance. H. 29.4 cm. EA 30735. COUNTERPOISES New Kingdom, *c*. 1350 BC; bronze, from Thebes. H. 14.5. cm. EA 20760 *and* Ptolemaic Period, 3rd century BC or later; bronze with polychrome glass inlay, of unknown provenance. H. 18 cm. EA 41515.

reunification under the governors of Thebes at the start of the second millennium B C; this seems an inadequate response to literature. It requires little imagination to realise that the descriptions of chaos, like the descriptions of order at the accession of a king, present in exaggerated style the world we live in, not historical catastrophe nor, in the case of the hymns to the accession of a king, cosmic miracle. The Egyptians lived as we do in a fragile world where order might dissolve into chaos at any moment if people did not exert themselves against it to their utmost; just as the desert sands could encroach on the valley margins, so the elements of chaos could intrude on the intricate web of human relations and social organisation that enable us to communicate with one another and to achieve ends. The opposite of a world falling apart was a world where things worked, and this ability to make things work was encapsulated in the word *menekh* which we rather feebly translate as 'efficacious'; a good king was a *menekh* king, one in whose reign everything went smoothly.

The core of the message of instructions, to do the right thing, found most concise expression in the laments of the eloquent forager. The laments form a series of exaggerated descriptions of disorder by a humble trader from the margins of the land, the Wadi Natrun between valley fields and empty desert; on his way to the

79 Stela of the royal scribe and cupbearer Hori, shown adoring the enthroned king Ramses IV who holds the *ankh* symbol of life and behind whom stands the goddess Maat. She is in the guise of a woman and is crowned with a feather, the hieroglyph used to write the word *maat*, 'what is right', and she has outstretched wings in a protective embrace around the king. The stela represents in graphic form the two blessings offered by the State in return for obedient service: life (security) and right (justice), the two features used to legitimate all states. 20th Dynasty, *c.* 1150 BC; limestone, from Deir el-Medina, Thebes. H. 76 cm. EA 588.

markets of the big city the trader is robbed of his wares by an estate official, and takes his case to the landowner, the High Steward of the king. In a curiously self-conscious denial of basic justice, the king has the man from the Wadi Natrun detained in order to extract from him as many petitions as possible, because the man speaks more eloquently than any ever heard before. At the end of the ninth petition the exhausted and desperate tradesman declaims:

> *There is no yesterday for the withdrawn man*
> *There is no friend for the deaf man,*
> *there is no happy day for the grasping-hearted.*

These three statements summarise all the social teaching of the instructions in negative form as expounded by Jan Assman. If a man does not act sociably, he has no 'yesterday', in other words he has broken the social bond that dictates that what is done yesterday should be repaid today, that actions should be linked across time. If a man does not communicate and is deaf to the words of others, then he has no 'friend', because he gives and receives nothing in the social give and take of day-to-day communication, day-to-day life. If a man is greedy and grasping, he has no 'happy day', in Egyptian a phrase for merrymaking and festive eating, drinking and music. If a person thinks only to save his goods for himself and never shares in the social spirit of giving for nothing, of 'wasting' good resources on social gatherings to have a good time, then that person cuts himself out of the community in which enjoyment of life depends in no small part on displays of generosity. All these negations of what is right help to delineate precisely what Right meant to the Egyptians, a vision of life which perhaps more than any other aspect links the Pharaonic world to our own.

The similarities with the ancient world should not blind us to the differences. Egyptian society was structured even more hierarchically than our own, and the texts, produced within the confines of the élite who alone could read and write, include many that enjoin upon the individual a deferential attitude to authority that can appear servile to the modern reader. Many texts of kingship insist on the self-abasement of subjects, a trait that finds outright visual expression in depictions of the court under Akhenaten. It is a sign of the high respect accorded to human beings that traditional representations of the same scene, while placing the king at the centre and on a far larger scale to match his solar divinity, nevertheless present human subjects without demeaning their dignity. From this human dignity flowed their social being, producing another difference between modern European tradition and the Egyptian legacy, that is the placing of society before the individual; when Ramses III is made to describe the chaos before his reign in the Great Harris Papyrus, his words include the disapproving remark 'every man was his own judge', in other words that each individual decided his own values for himself, precisely the ideal goal for life according to modern ideas. The Egyptians viewed such individuality not as a virtue but as a mark of selfishness that denied to the community its central role and threatened existence with catastrophe.

A third fundamental difference lay in the extension of the community to include the dead. Festivals included those on which the family visited dead relatives to feast with them at the family grave and the great tomb-chapels of outstanding members of the richer families provided a monumental setting for those occasions. Belief in the community of living and dead emerges most solidly in the letters to the dead; little more than a dozen have survived, but they range in date from the late third to the late second millennium BC and in place from southern Upper Egypt to Memphis at the threshold of the Delta, and seem thus to be derived from a nation-wide belief that persisted across the centuries. In these letters a person appealed directly to a recently deceased close relative to thwart forces that were causing misery in life. Although the surviving stock includes examples on papyrus like ordinary letters in the world of the living, the writer could try to ensure that the letter was read by writing it on the pottery vessels used to place food offerings at the tomb. All surviving letters deal with domestic complaints such as illness or discord between members of the household. In the Ptolemaic Period the letter to the dead was replaced by letters to the patron deities of the local necropolis, but these reveal the same perennial concerns.

Letters to the living also demonstrate where Egyptians placed their trust. From $c.$ 2000 to 1200 BC the introductory formulae tend to name the prominent national and local deities, and the standard formula for assuring the recipient that the writer is well runs 'I am well today, and do not know my condition of tomorrow'. Later letters give similar introductory formulae but present the future as in the hands of the creator, 'I am well today, tomorrow is in the hands of god'. Some of the later letters include prayers for the welfare of the writer as well as for that of the recipient, as most emphatically in the missive of a father to his son, an official in the administration of the Theban necropolis, $c.$ 1050 BC, sent from the depths of Nubia; there the Pharaoh's general was campaigning against a rebel viceroy of Kush and the father asks his son to pray to the Theban deities Amun, Merseger, king Amenhotep, queen Ahmose Nefertari and Hathor to 'bring him back in good health, to let him come down home to Egypt from the distant land where he is'. Instructions too show a change in emphasis, moving from the civil or secular, as we might class it, advice of the early second millennium BC – when texts advise a man how to succeed in life by playing the appointed part in the fixed hierarchies – to the later instructions of Any and Amenemipet, of the fourteenth and eleventh centuries BC respectively, which equate wisdom with piety and come close to the spirit of the Hebrew Psalms, in some cases possibly even reflecting direct contacts.

Prayers and hymns are attested throughout the Pharaonic Period but these also take on a new character from the fourteenth century BC, with direct acknowledgements of guilt and dedications of the person and property to a deity. There is a considerable difference between earlier monuments and texts, written in the classic idiom which we name Middle Egyptian, and the later parallels, sometimes in the less formal idiom of Late Egyptian. Yet the difference seems more one of expression and style than of substance. Earlier texts acknowledge dependence on the gods in a more refined or at least less extended vein, though it is nonetheless present, nowhere more so than in the very names of individuals such as Saamun, 'son of Amun', or Senusret, 'man of the mighty goddess'. The Ramesside and later texts have been given the label 'personal piety', but this seems a tautologous designation that ascribes to earlier periods a lack of both personal access to the divine and personal reverence for the divine. It is important not to draw too heavy a line between later and earlier expressions of belief, and equally important to compare like with like; if there are fewer earlier texts that we might class devotional, this may in part reflect the court-bound character of early writing in Egypt where written texts appear in the confines of the first royal court of all Egypt $c.$ 3000 BC, then move away from the ruling administrative class only a thousand years later, and even in the latest periods remained confined to a minority.

At court, devotion was due first to the ruler and the king protected the weak directly, pre-empting in theory the need for any other divine intervention. With the withdrawal of the king from Thebes in the New Kingdom, an area that produced texts, a space opened for a less élite view of divine action. Even in the new structure of belief, it should be noted that the men claiming Amun as the helper of the poor were themselves among the richest in the land and that the devices of the later texts were as impersonal and formulaic in most instances as the phrasing of traditional hymns and prayers. If we compare like with like, for example texts within the same genre, the distinct feature of the later texts lies in the phrasing, particularly among Ramesside hieroglyphic monuments from the community of royal craftsmen working on the tombs of the Ramesside kings at Thebes. These represent a new emphasis on the paternal and direct involvement of deities in human life, but do not replace the older types of text; they manifest a new readiness to resort to the divine in daily life, but that relation may always have been present below the world of the text in earlier ages. The later type of texts should therefore be classed as devotional texts, a group expressing a different character within the same general scheme of linking humanity to the gods. The devotional prayers and hymns occur on tomb-chapel walls and stelae to record the connection of the individual to a deity, perhaps most fully in the inscriptions of Samut Kyky, a man who made over his entire estate to the goddess Mut; the name and the text of this man present both the earlier and the later demonstration of dependence upon the divine.

Devotional texts on stelae sometimes record events in which the power of a deity manifests itself in the interest of justice, as perhaps most famously in the stela of Neferabut, one of the Theban craftsmen of the royal tomb; the front side of the stela shows Neferabut kneeling in adoration of Ptah with the words of a hymn to the god, while the back contains a poetic account of disaster that befell this and doubtless many other ancient artists.

> *Beginning of the account of the powers of Ptah-south-of-his-wall by the servant in the Place of Right (the royal necropolis) on the west of Thebes Neferabu(t), true of voice. He says:*
>
> *I am the man who swore falsely by Ptah lord of Right;*
> *he caused me to see darkness by day,*
> *I will recount his powers to the one who does not know him and to the one who knows him, to lesser and great.*
> *Beware Ptah lord of Right,*
> *see, he has not set down (?) the misdeed of anyone.*

> *Dread pronouncing the name of Ptah in wrong;*
> *see, the one who pronounced it in wrong, see, he is overthrown.*
> *He caused me to be like the hounds of the street;*
> *I am in his hand.*
> *He caused people and gods to see in me that I am like a man who has committed a*
> *crime against his master.*
> *Ptah lord of Right is in the right against me.*
> *he has made for me a lesson.*
> *Show mercy to me. May I see your mercy.*

The stela inscription of Qenherkhepeshef, another royal craftsman at Thebes, presents a more general account of devotional deeds in the thirteenth century BC:

> *I have walked in the Place of Beauty (the Valley of the Queens).*
> *I have spent the night in this forecourt.*
> *I have drunk the water sent (by the god?) and extended in the forecourt of*
> *Menet; it waters the plants and lotus-flowers in the forecourt of Ptah.*
> *My body has spent the night in the shadow of your face.*
> *I have slept in your forecourt.*
> *I have made stelae in the temple beside the lords of Djeseret (Deir el-Bahri).*
> *For the* ka *of one excellent and exact, a fashioner of images of all deities, servant*
> *in the Place of Right Qenherkhepeshef.*

The reference to sleeping in a temple is particularly intriguing because Qenherkhepeshef was the stepson of the owner of the Book of Dreams cited above; no other evidence survives for the soliciting of dreams before the Ptolemaic Period.

Similar devotional texts appear in the same period, the thirteenth and twelfth centuries BC, among literary compositions on ostraca and in longer selections on papyrus. An example on one of a group of literary papyri probably from the necropolis of Memphis demonstrates the imagery of devoted man before protective deity that runs through the genre:

> *Pilot who knows the water, Amun, [unswerving] rudder,*
> *the one who gives bread to the man without,*
> *who sustains the servant of his house.*
> *I make myself no official as my protector,*
> *I mix with no lord of plenty, . . .*
> *My divine lord is protector, I know his might,*
> *for the protector is the strong-armed god,*
> *only he alone is strong.*
> *Amun who knows the reticent,*
> *he who hears the one who calls to him,*
> *Amun-Ra king of the gods,*
> *the bull strong of arm, beloved for his arm.*

80 The stela of Qenherkhepshef shown in adoration of the goddess Hathor who is enthroned and has an *ankh* symbol of life in attendance as fan-bearer. 19th Dynasty, *c.* 1200 BC; limestone, from Deir el-Medina, Thebes. H. 19 cm. EA 278.

In this text the objection of Akhenaten to Amun becomes clear, for the supplicant treats the god of Thebes as protector in place of the king. The feature of turning to deities instead of to the king and the royal administration is today often seen as a major innovation of the period before and especially following Akhenaten, a trend that he tried to suppress but only succeeded in exacerbating. Certainly the bypassing of the king would not suit the tenor of royal texts, but it is important to note that those continue to exist alongside devotional texts, and that the novelty may be more in the expression of devotion than in its substance. New Kingdom Thebes fostered formal expression of the deity as king-like defender of the defenceless perhaps above all because Thebes in the New Kingdom had the status of a royal city but no resident king. The temple of Amun at Karnak received massive royal building programmes, but the king himself governed, as any ruler of all Egypt must, from the nodal point of Memphis or even farther to the north; Ramses II founded his new capital in the north-eastern Delta, and the successors of the Ramesside Pharaohs in the eleventh century BC moved downstream again to Tanis. The vacuum of royal presence in Thebes was filled by Amun and his temple became the southern branch of the administration for the convenience of the king; the proximity of the god became still more concrete in the great New Kingdom festivals at Thebes, the processions of the gods at the Valley and Ipet Festivals. When major and minor deities left their temples on processions, they became available as oracles to answer petitions on a more regular basis than the approach to the king on the royal progress through the land. In a city operating as a religious and artistic but not administrative or political capital, the tension between kingship and godhead would be intensified. In a community such as that of the craftsmen for the royal tomb, there would be additional space for views outside those held and voiced at the royal court. Together these Theban factors may have encouraged the movement to appeal to the gods in place of the king, although the new genre appears at other centres too, as in the Memphite papyrus cited above.

An example of ever-present feelings that only rarely found expression in the texts is scepticism. It is astonishing that the spirit of doubt ever found its way into the very monuments that immortalise in stone an unwavering faith in eternity. Doubt itself is as human and universal an emotion as faith, and none of us can escape either in our lives, although much of our lives are spent in the attempt; the inclusion of sceptical attitudes to the afterlife and to the funerary cult itself could only find space in the tomb within a general framework of faith – the belief that the monuments did have meaning, that it did make sense to build tomb-chapels, to bury the dead, to bring them offerings. The most often cited Egyptian text in this loophole of faith is the *Song of the Harpist from the chapel of king Intef*, a Middle Egyptian song surviving in a single Ramesside copy, where the refrain exhorts the living to make merry, for no-one can take their goods with them; the harpist observes that no-one has ever returned from the underworld to calm our hearts and tell us what death will be for us. No less remarkable is a stela set up for Tentimhotep, wife of the high priest of Ptah, in the reign of Cleopatra VII, the famous Cleopatra with whom the Macedonian dynasty of Ptolemy came to its dramatic end; scepticism and faith combine in breathtaking unison as the young woman describes her prayers for a son, the dream in which Ptah promised her husband a son in return for work on his sanctuary, and their joy at the birth, followed by the lament from which these closing extracts are taken:

> *O my brother, my husband, friend, high priest,*
> *tire not of drink and food, of quaffing deep, of loving! . . .*
> *The west, it is a land of sleep, . . .*
> *The water of life which has food for all, it is thirst for me;*
> *it comes to the one on earth, while I thirst with water beside me . . .*
> *As to death, 'Come!' is his name,*
> *all whom he summons come to him immediately,*
> *their hearts in fear through dread of him.*
> *Of gods and men no-one beholds him,*
> *yet great and less are in his hand . . .*
> *O all you who come to this burial place,*
> *give me incense upon the fire,*
> *and water on every festival of the west.*

5

SURVIVING DEATH

Transfiguration

ANCIENT EGYPTIANS STAND ACCUSED in modern minds of being obsessed with death in a morbid and ultimately unconvincing manner. In part the climate of the land is to blame, as the cemeteries in the desert survive so much better than the towns in the fertile valley where changes in the course of the Nile and reuse by new centres of population can obliterate once flourishing sites. Europe too might seem preoccupied with death if only cemeteries survived, particularly the monumental labyrinths of the nineteenth century at Highgate in London or Père Lachaise in Paris or the vast war cemeteries of the twentieth century. Nevertheless the Egyptians did build their houses for the living of brick and those for the dead of stone, and their art and literature do bear the strong imprint of the tomb-chapel. One central observation may be made in their defence, quite aside from our own negative obsession with death that seeks to exclude the subject entirely and unrealistically from our own world. The Egyptians were interested not in death itself but in an afterlife and they stocked both burial chamber and tomb-chapel with the bounty of this world, the obvious and immediate focus of their living attention. Death was not an enemy or an obstacle but a doorway to another existence; the aim of the Egyptian was not our foolish aim of not dying but the more poignant hope of not repeating death, of finding beyond death the life that they could enjoy so fully on this side.

Our difficulties with Egyptian funerary customs stem largely from the very point of departure, the practice of placing goods in the grave. This practice is present from the moment that the ancestors of the Pharaohs settled to farm in the Nile Valley *c*. 4000 BC, and indeed burial goods remain the major source of information

81 Stela of Khamuy showing him seated at a table of offerings and with the designation 'excellent *akh*-spirit of Ra' to reinforce the identity of the man as a fully operational being after death. The roundel at the top is decorated with *wedjat*-eyes, a *shen*-ring, water and a water vessel as symbols of the daily circuit of the sun. 19th Dynasty, *c*. 1250 BC; limestone, from Deir el-Medina, Thebes. H. 19 cm. EA 344.

on the fourth millennium BC. The presence of food offerings in particular implies a continued material use of human faculties after death for offerings require of the deceased both an ability to eat and drink, that is to absorb energy from food and liquid after death as in life, and to move to the place with the offerings, even if this were only a few metres away. Throughout the Pharaonic Period the two forms of surviving death, the spirit of sustenance and the spirit of mobility, shared the task of perpetuating existence for the individual. If the insistence on the physical after-life seems to us preposterous, it should be noted that the Egyptians witnessed the physical survival of the body with their own eyes; fourth-millennium burials directly in the sand preserve even today the skin and hair as well as the bones, giving a skeleton something approaching its former condition in life.

This simple natural desiccation in the sand preserved the body without human intervention, but the introduction of reed matting and then of square wooden box-coffins removed the dead from the preserving work of the desert. Rather than abandon the use of coffins, such an important show of status and so powerful a means of protecting the deceased, the Egyptians spent the rest of their ancient history trying to achieve the same goal as Saharan desiccation. They first began to

82 OPPOSITE Stela of a man named Hor shown adoring a mummiform falcon headed Ra-Horakhty. The table of offerings between them shows clearly how both gods and the dead depended on an eternal supply of food and drink offerings for sustenance. Late Period, after 600 BC; limestone, of unknown provenance. H. 39 cm. EA 639.

83 BELOW A body desiccated by the sand and preserving, in addition to the bones, much of the skin and some of the linen and reed covering of the body. Late Predynastic Period, c.3500 BC; from Gebelein. L. 1.49 m. EA 32753.

develop a method of embalming the dead by the start of the third millennium and this they had perfected two thousand years later and continued to employ into the Roman Period, albeit at a less technically impressive standard. The main ingredient was dry natron, a disinfectant and desiccating agent found in Egypt, at the Wadi Natrun for example. By packing the bodies in dry natron, the Egyptians found that they could arrest decay; the removal of the internal organs also helped. The dried body was washed, wrapped in strips of old linen and deluged in resins and oils, giving a final blackened appearance resembling pitch. From the external appearance the early travellers accepted the Arabic term *mummiya*, 'bitumen', said to be of Persian derivation; embalmed bodies are called mummies and the process mummification, even though the blackening of the body was caused by resin and other plant and animal oils and unguents, bitumen itself not being applied until a late date. Mummification combines a physical preservation of the body, to keep it the same, with the anticipation of a spiritual afterlife, to transfigure the person and make him or her new and different, 'radiant'. Since the efforts to preserve a lifelike outer appearance can only be said to be partially successful, they were supplemented by plaster modelling of facial features and limbs in the third millennium and by packing the skin with stuffing in the early first millennium B C. The art of embalming reached its creative peak in Thebes in the eleventh and tenth centuries B C; in the Ptolemaic and Roman Periods stress was lain instead on the neat outer wrapping of the bandages, often concealing an alarming assortment of limbs within. Throughout this history the body would be adorned with a variety of figures, as in life, to protect and enhance its vitality; the most common such amulets were the *wedjat* or eye of wholesomeness, the *djed*-pillar of stability and figures of deities.

From *c.*2000 B C the head might be covered with a mask made of linen layers stiffened with plaster, a papier mâché effect called cartonnage. In later periods the mask might be of other materials, the most celebrated being the inlaid gold mask of Tutankhamun (fourteenth century B C). The cartonnage mask may have spurred the development of anthropoid coffins in place of the earlier box-coffins, since the earliest coffins in mummy form, in the nineteenth century B C, could be made of cartonnage as well as wood, the more common material for the type. In the later second millennium B C openwork cartonnage covers were sometimes laid over the mummified body, and in the ninth to eighth centuries B C and again in the Ptolemaic Period the wooden coffin was replaced by a cartonnage case that entirely enclosed the mummy. From the fourteenth century B C the stone sarcophagus containing the body and coffins in the richest burials might also be mummiform; the earliest example is that of Merymose, the viceroy of Nubia under Amenhotep III. In all of these adaptations of the body-container to resemble the body, the head plays the crucial role that it had already in the twenty-sixth to twenty-fifth centuries B C; at that time a sculpted head of the individual might be placed in a burial as if to secure possession of the head should the original be damaged. The precise function of these 'reserve heads' cannot be determined in the absence of texts and insufficient archaeological information about the exact place of the sculpted head in the burial place but speculation ranges from the notion that the sculpture identified the burial

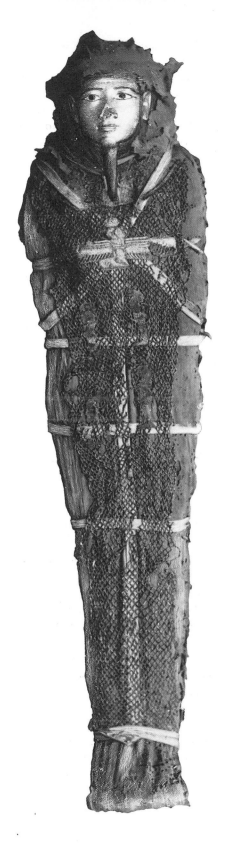

84 Wrapped mummified body from the coffin of
Irethoreru, equipped with a gilt mask which
includes the divine beard and covered in a bead
netting with a figure of Nut over the breast.
26th Dynasty, $c.600$ BC (?); from Akhmim.
L. 1.65 m. EA 20745.

for the wandering spirit of the dead person, to the proposition that the head gave the deceased vision of the heavenly forces for its regeneration. The funerary literature includes incantations to prevent the head of a man being taken from him in the afterlife.

The most constant feature of burials across the three millennia of Pharaonic history is the coffin, the only object other than pottery and human remains to be attested at all places and all times. The earliest coffins were square box-shapes, a form adapted to a rectangle once the process of mummification had required that the body be stretched out for embalming after death. At the earliest stage coffin and tomb present a house for eternity for the dead and some thirtieth-century BC examples are equipped with model estate or with boats for transport next to the tomb-chapel. From $c.2800$ BC rectangular coffins become the norm for wealthy burials, with a continuous motif of the niched façade, embodying defence and

85 BELOW Rectangular coffin of the type predominant in Old and Middle Kingdom burials, the end of the history of this type. At that time the outer sides of the coffin were adorned with a false door and $wedjat$-eyes at the point where the head of the deceased might look out. An elaborate panelled 'palace facade' motif, deriving ultimately from Early Dynastic building facades, also decorated the coffin. The insides of these types bear no texts other than the offering formula. This example was made as stock rather than to order and the space for the name is filled with its purchaser, the priest Amenhotep. Second Intermediate Period, $c.1600$ BC; painted wood, from Thebes. L. 2 m. EA 12270.

86 OPPOSITE From the mid-12th Dynasty the Egyptians began to make inner coffins in the form of a wrapped mummy with an unwrapped face, evoking the mummy with mummy-mask. It was at first used for inner coffins which had an outer rectangular coffin, but in the New Kingdom it ousted the rectangular coffin as the principal shape for mummy-containers. This face from an anthropoid coffin demonstrates the heights of the artistry of sculptors in wood at the funerary workshops. 18th Dynasty, $c.1400$ BC; wood with inlaid eyes of obsidian, ivory and bronze, of unknown provenance. H. 23 cm. EA 6887.

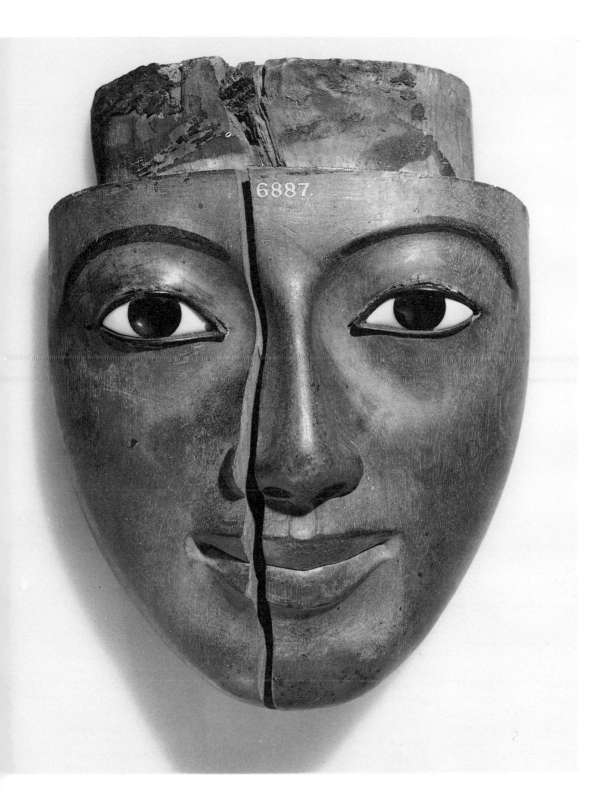

87, 88 and 89 Each funerary cult involved acts and speech of ritual that survive only indirectly in the scenes and objects for the cult. The coffin of Hor (ABOVE) includes a scene of the funerary priest reciting the offering formula with his fist clenched in a particular gesture, with the deceased represented as a man at the table of offerings which has been stylised into vertical loaves to evoke the Field of Reeds where crops were cultivated in the afterlife. The Old Kingdom set of metal vessels (OPPOSITE, TOP) and calcite tray for the seven prescribed sacred oils (OPPOSITE, BOTTOM) represent the tools of the funerary priest's trade, in this case inscribed for the benefit of a lector-priest named Idi. COFFIN 26th Dynasty, $c.650$ BC; painted wood, from Thebes. L. 2.13 m. EA 15655. METAL TABLE OF VESSELS 6th Dynasty, $c.2300$ BC; copper, from Abydos. H. 16.7 cm. EA 5315. SLAB FOR OILS 6th Dynasty, $c.2300$ BC; calcite, from Abydos. W. 13 cm. EA 6123.

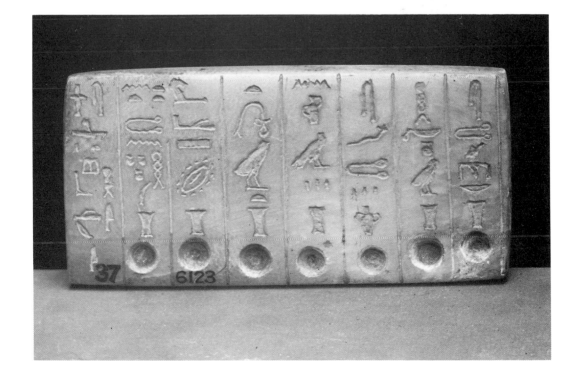

found in the enclosure walls of both palace and tombs in the first centuries after unification. In the late third millennium BC a pair of eyes over a 'false door' was added at what would be the east side of the north end of the coffin when oriented in the burial chamber, to allow the deceased access to the offerings in the tomb-chapel. On these earliest coffins the texts present the formula for an eternal supply of offerings. From $c.2000$ BC the texts extend to funerary literature, and in the following century the anthropoid coffin makes its entry as an inner coffin within an outer rectangular coffin. The subsequent periods saw the anthropoid coffin maintained, and decoration reaching a peak of intricacy in the Theban coffins of the eleventh and tenth centuries BC, while the outer rectangular coffin, like the stone sarcophagus, was provided only for the richest burials at certain periods and varied in shape from anthropoid to chest-form. Other objects might be placed around the body or coffin, the custom varying from one period to the next. The late Old Kingdom and early Middle Kingdom burial chambers without decorated tomb-chapels housed wooden models of work on estates, late Middle Kingdom burial chambers contained figures of animals and the ivory markers wielded against demons at birth or in pregnancy, while New Kingdom burial chambers preserved items from the houses of the living, particularly where the message of rejuvenation might be prominent, as in mirrors and cosmetic vessels with figures of young girls, mothers and children, or particular animals and birds such as fox and duck. The details of symbolism await further research, but in each case it is important to remember that the ancient Egyptians did not divide the tomb-complex as thoroughly as time and we ourselves have done; despite the rarity of surviving tomb-groups, it is essential to see each as a unity comprising body adornments, coffin and sarcophagus decoration, items in the burial chamber and the tomb-chapel above ground. If any of these is not present, its absence should be taken into account either as part of the original arrangement of the group or, to complicate research, as a result of the imperfections in the surviving record. Texts and images would have been able to complement one another, and one item might find its complement in another; thus in the tomb of Thutmose III, the *Litany of Ra* occupies part of the shroud over the body of the king, but is completed on pillars in a chamber of the tomb. The texts require special attention as an articulation of the aims of funerary practice in verbal form, and they are taken separately for that reason, though it is stressed that they belong in the architectural context of the tomb as part of the mechanism to bring a body to eternal life.

90 Stela of Tjatayu from an offering-chapel at Abydos, showing him before a table of offerings adoring Ra-Horakhty beneath the winged sun-disk. Like many owners of stelae at that site, Tjatayu held a position in the local temple, in this case as head barber of the Osiris domain; he would have been responsible for shaving the heads of priests, a requirement for entering the sanctuary. After the 26th Dynasty, Abydos and its Osiris temple became eclipsed by the growth of the nearby centre of Akhmim, particularly after the foundation of the new port of Ptolemais. 26th Dynasty, $c.650$ BC; painted limestone, from Abydos. H. 40 cm. EA 1317.

The division of text from context becomes particularly artificial when we consider the practicalities of mummification. No clear division emerges in Egyptian-language sources between those reciting the texts or performing the rites and those carrying out the physical treatment of the body; Ptolemaic documents in Greek and the Greek historian Herodotus distinguish two categories of embalmer, *paraschistes*, 'slitter', and *taricheutes*, 'pickler', and the later Greek writer Diodorus explains that the former cut open the body, to be ritually chased away by the other embalmers, the 'picklers'. Yet even the Greek-language distinction need not imply a division of physical and verbal labour, since the act of cutting open the body to permit retrieval of soft inner organs was as much a ritualised action as any other, equated with the murder of Osiris by Seth, and both Greek terms 'split' and 'pickle' imply physical treatment. The Egyptian texts offer more decorous terms, placing the art of embalming on a level with healing and with the reading and enacting of other ritual texts; the terms 'physician', 'lector-priest' and 'embalmer' become interchangeable in late first-millennium BC texts. In its setting in life the mummifying of the body unites word and deed, forming a seamless flow in burial, from the laying of the body in the embalming workshop to its placing in the tomb. The surviving human remains, burial equipment and funerary texts amount to mere tangible remnants of that single social act of burying the dead.

The first texts and images produced to secure a good life after death concerned provisioning the deceased and were set into chapels above the tombs of courtiers. In the early period of unification *c.* 3000–2600 BC they were single stone slabs with the name, titles and representation of the deceased, while more elaborate examples were accompanied by an offering table and listing of material goods to be supplied to the tomb in perpetuity. The texts expanded to justify the existence of first the tomb and then, in the later third millennium BC, the tomb-owner himself, and to give his career as well as his titles. The depictions expanded at the same time to cover in the richest instances, after *c.* 2600 BC, the entire interior wall surface of a tomb-chapel, providing an elaborate account of the provisioning for an estate. The chapel for the cult of the deceased involved both the craftsmen and, inextricably, the ritual specialists who brought two- and three-dimensional images to life to perform their eternal material tasks, a double act of creation and so of cost available only to the dominant strata of society. Such chapels were set up over the burial place or, more rarely, on other sites selected for their funerary sanctity, above all Abydos as the burial place of Osiris. The persistence of chapel-building into the Ptolemaic Period, when some of the finest hieroglyphic stelae were executed, demonstrates the strength of social belief in the sustenance of the spirit; the strand of scepticism voiced as one genre of funerary lament (see the end of chapter four) never came to supplant the role model of Osiris and aspirations for everlasting life, as it has done in Europe.

Until the end of the third millennium BC the written and pictorial record for others than the king concerned the *ka*, the sustaining spirit of the body. The first funerary texts that expound on the freedom of the dead to move were inscribed *c.* 2500 BC on the walls of the chambers within the pyramid of Unas, in a matching of text contents to wall-space logical to a degree rarely attained in the later pyramids of the millennium, though those too were inscribed with texts to secure the regeneration and eternal life of the king. As with all later funerary literature these so-called *Pyramid Texts* record a variety of extracts from different sources otherwise lost to us, from the corpus of incantations against harmful creatures to the ritual pronouncements accompanying offerings to excerpts of kingly and other rituals to passages composed for the funeral ceremony itself. For the pyramid of Unas Jürgen Osing has demonstrated the links between the texts and their architectural setting on the following pattern.

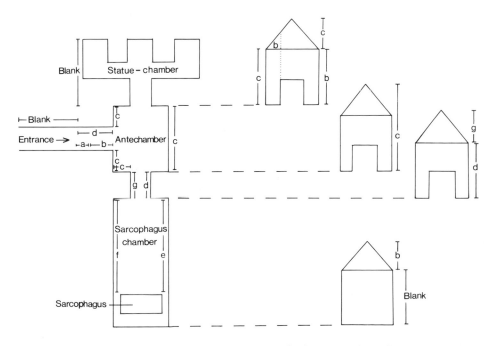

a Appearance of the dead king, sometimes in animal form, among the gods

b Incantations against snakes

c For ascent to the sky

d For an afterlife, especially as an imperishable spirit

e For an afterlife, identifying limbs of the dead king with limbs of various deities

f Offering list

g Accompanying text to offering list

The entrance to the antechamber is marked by a group of texts which place the king among night and day deities, particularly in animal form; these follow a text for opening the sky and the earliest incantation against harmful creatures; other texts against snakes are positioned at the western and eastern ends of the area inscribed, again with clear defensive intent. One among the texts on the western gable wards off scorpions as well as serpents:

The head of the great bull is severed.
Viper, I tell you this,
scorpion, I tell you this.
Overturn yourself, squirm into the ground before me.
I tell you this.

The northern wall of the sarcophagus chamber bears the great offering list and the adjacent surfaces carry its accompanying text, the only place where the dead king is consistently addressed as the Osiris Unas. The offering list links each type of offering to the eye of Horus, with frequent resort to the surface similarities between words; these the Egyptians viewed, not in our analytic manner as coincidence or as the result of different formations from the same root, but as the embodiment of an ever-present divine order, incarnate in the sacred script so deeply that the hieroglyphs themselves were called not signs but 'words of god'. An example such as the following is thus not a playful pun but a calculated entwining of the material world with the world of the gods:

Osiris Unas
receive the eye of Horus which he has saved (shed) *from Seth:*
(offering-) *two bowls of* ished-*fruit.*

Both offering list and incantations against intruding creatures appear in the same versions within royal pyramids of the next three centuries. The other texts in the pyramids vary considerably more, but present the same aims of preserving, sustaining and giving freedom to the deceased king. In the sarcophagus chamber the texts concentrate on obtaining an afterlife as an 'excellent imperishable spirit'. Nearest the sarcophagus in which the king lay the texts identify each part of his body with the corresponding part of a deity, a technique for avoiding bodily decay found also in texts for healing the living.

O Unas, you are not departed dead,
you have departed alive to be seated on the throne of Osiris,
with your sceptre in your hand, you issue commands to the living.
See, your staff has been installed in your hand.
Issue commands to the most secret of places!
Your upper arm is that of Atum, your forearms are those of Atum,
your belly is that of Atum, your back is that of Atum,
your rear is that of Atum, your legs are those of Atum,
your face is that of Anubis.
The mounds of Horus revolve for you,
the mounds of Seth revolve for you.

Here at the western end of the chambers the king is incorporated into the solar cycle of rebirth, where the sun-god is named Ra-Atum. The antechamber texts aim to secure ascent to the sky with or without reference to the sun-god, here named simply Ra. One of the most dramatic images of the dead king incorporating the powers of the gods has him devouring them:

> The sky darkens, the stars are obscured,
> the bows (i.e. lands) tremble, the bones of the Earth-lion quake and they cease from movement,
> when they have seen Unas arisen as the god
> who lives on his fathers, who feeds on his mothers.

More typical is the incantation for ferrying the king to the sky:

> Wake in peace, you whose face is behind, in peace,
> you who see behind, in peace, ferryman of the sky, in peace,
> ferryman of Nut, in peace, ferryman of the gods, in peace.
> Unas has come to you that you may ferry him in that ferry with which you ferry the gods.

The guarantee for everlasting life was sought with Osiris in the food of the earth and in the sky with the imperishable stars and the sun. These traits stayed with funerary texts to the end of the Egyptian tradition and the *Pyramid Texts* themselves continued in use, albeit in extracts and modified versions, throughout this span of two and a half thousand years. Towards the end of the third millennium there also appeared a new corpus of texts that laid greater emphasis on the afterlife beneath the earth in the kingdom of Osiris in which the deceased farmed the miraculously large harvests of the Fields of Offerings and of Rushes. The new funerary corpus was written most often in cursive hieroglyphs on the sides of coffins instead of burial chamber walls, and for that reason is now called the *Coffin Texts*. The earliest examples survive as faint signs on plaster, possibly the impressions from a shroud, on the fragments of a coffin found in 1978–9 around the body of Medunefer in his tomb at Balat, in the Dakhla oasis. Medunefer held the title of governor of the oasis in the reign of Pepy II or shortly after, the very time at which the *Pyramid Texts* of the king were adopted in the tombs of queens in the Memphite necropolis.

The relaxation of the kingly prerogative extended still further in the following century when *Pyramid Texts* began to appear on non-royal coffins, and a high official of the twentieth century BC even had his burial chamber inscribed with the *Pyramid Texts* of Unas. The adoption of royal texts and images by people other than kings is termed 'democratisation' in Egyptology and is usually said to relate to the degeneration of the kingdom into disunity in the late third millennium BC. Yet there are difficulties with the label, quite apart from the anachronistic use of the Greek concepts of *demos*, 'the (male) citizenry', and 'democracy', 'rule by the citizens'. Motifs of kingship were taken up by ordinary mortals at two periods in particular, the ends of the third and of the second millennium BC, but at neither period do we have funerary texts of contemporary kings with which to compare

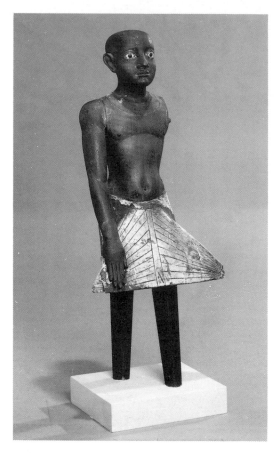

91 and 92 Examples of breach and maintenance of kingly prerogatives. The figurine represents a man who is not a king, as he wears no uraeus but has adopted the royal *shendyt*-kilt; by contrast the demon statue belongs to a type known exclusively from the royal tombs in the Valley of the Kings. With an imperfect surviving record it is often difficult to detect exactly how firmly the distinction between king and subjects was being maintained at any given time. FIGURINE Late Middle Kingdom, *c.*1750 BC (?); wood with gilt kilt and necklace and inlaid eyes, of unknown provenance. H. excluding modern legs 21 cm. EA 56842. DEMON 19th Dynasty, *c.*1225 BC; wood with traces of resin covering, from the Valley of the Kings, Thebes. H. of figure 42.5 cm, H. of base 8.2 cm. The base is a Late Period plinth for an Osiris statue attached to the figure by the 19th-century discoverer of the two items, and comes from a different part of the Theban necropolis. EA 61283.

them and so we do not know whether or not the difference between kingly and other burials was maintained at those times. If new texts had been devised for the king, relaxation of the royal monopoly on the older texts would not lessen the gap between king and subjects. In a few cases we find kingly texts in non-kingly tombs at periods when those texts were still reserved for the king, as in the pyramids of queens in the late third millennium BC and the burial chambers of the highest officials of Hatshepsut and Thutmose III, yet those exceptions fall within the innermost court circles and, as tokens of exceptional royal favour, would have

strengthened as much as weakened the throne by demonstrating the power of the sovereign to reward especially beloved subjects. Furthermore, although the texts for Thutmose III survive, those for Hatshepsut do not, again complicating efforts to estimate the difference between kingly and other funerary literature.

The Ramesside Period produced at least three breaches of royal monopoly on texts which cannot be ascribed to favour within the court: a royal archivist Khay adapted for himself the text of the *King as Priest of the Sun* in his funerary papyrus; a third priest of Amun Tjanefer incorporated excerpts from one of the royal *Underworld Books* (see below) into the decoration of his tomb-chapel; Anhay, a woman with high priestly offices used the same source for part of her funerary papyrus. All three are Theban sources and their existence may testify to a relaxation in royal power and interest in Thebes. Although this development may seem to undermine the distinction between king and subjects, it is important to note that Tjanefer and Anhay probably date to the reign of Ramses III, one of the mightiest of Pharaohs.

The use of insignia and texts of kings in non-royal funerary equipment to a great extent confirms rather than subverts the central role of the office of king in ancient Egypt. The usage goes beyond the adage that imitation is the sincerest form of flattery for the stake here is eternal life. If the subjects of the king laid no store by the power of kingship, they would scarcely have taken up the model provided by royal texts for the promise of a good afterlife. The label 'democratisation' thus reverses the historical direction of the trend; the 'people' do not intrude into royal power, on the contrary the role of king intrudes into the burial customs not of the 'people', but of those subjects who were sufficiently well placed to commission for their tombs and chapels texts and images for the afterlife. In a land where writing came into existence in the service of the king it is not surprising that the first funerary texts should be those for the king; it is equally natural that the king, as incarnation of the sun-god, should be deemed to hold uniquely intimate knowledge of the solar cycle with which he would at death be reunited and of the realm of Osiris with whom he became identical when his successor became the living son Horus. Such a powerful bond of regeneration on earth and in heaven corresponded fluently to the double survival of body and person, and thus offered a perfect pattern on which funerary texts for others than the king could be modelled when they came into existence later. It should be emphasised that the use of royal motifs for others than the king remained strictly confined to the tomb and so to aspirations for the afterlife; the king's subjects aimed, in these texts and images, to become one with the two supreme deities of the afterlife, Ra and Osiris, and kingship offered a way.

In the absence of royal funerary literature the *Coffin Texts* form the sole survivors in the genre for the period 2000–1600 B C. The most productive area, as far as can be judged from the evidence today, lay not at the ancient royal city of Memphis or at Thebes, the hometown of the governors who reunited Egypt, but halfway between the two in the area of Middle Egypt, at Siut, Meir, Beni Hasan and above all Bersha. In these cemeteries the local governors and other members of leading families were able to construct great rock-cut tombs and tomb-chapels around which the tombs of their provincial courtiers could cluster. Bersha, necropolis of Khemenu (Hermopolis/Ashmunein), yielded coffins of exceptional craftsmanship, the finest made of imported cedarwood, with texts that comprise the richest tradition of the period; it may be no accident that Khemenu was cult centre of Thoth, god of knowledge, above all of written knowledge. The encoded knowledge of the afterlife on Bersha *Coffin Texts* includes the earliest known map, a guide for the deceased to the lands ruled by Osiris. Egyptologists call this map and accompanying texts the *Book of Two Ways* because it presents two paths to new life. It is possible that one path was of fire, the other of water, but the two elements can represent two aspects of the same entity, like the divine force that rages as Sekhmet and is content as Hathor; thus the Island of Fire in the afterlife is said in the texts to consume the wicked in flames but to provide the good with refreshing water.

The Bersha texts also preserve compositions concerning the unfurling of creation, as cited in chapter one. One example describes the creator in a poem interspersed with commentary, and is the most common surviving *Coffin Text*, found on coffins from all the main cemeteries of the period, sometimes with the title 'incantation for going out (of the tomb) by day in the necropolis'. The title became used for each entire series of funerary texts after 1500 BC, the corpus we call the *Book of the Dead*, in which the old text continued to appear as one of the most frequently copied compositions until the Roman Period. In the form used in the late second millennium the title for this text sometimes opens with or includes the word *sakhu*, 'transfigurations', texts to transform a person into an *akh*. The word *akh* and its offshoots cover a range of reference from *akhet*, 'horizon', to *akh*, 'be useful [to someone]', but the core meaning encapsulates the concept of light, and the *akh* is the transfigured spirit that has become one with the light. The opposite of *akh* is *mut*, 'dead', the person who had died and not been transfigured. Letters to the dead address deceased relatives as *akh*, 'transfigured spirit', and identify harmful spirits that cause strife in the world as *mut*, 'the dead', by implication the dead that remain dead after death and fail to attain a good afterlife. The closest analogies in modern languages would be the 'blessed dead' for *akh*, and the 'damned' for *mut*. Therefore *sakhu*, 'transfigurations', embody the very core of purpose in funerary literature, the quest to be one with the forces of light and to escape eternal darkness. It is the title given in the fourth century BC to series of *Pyramid Texts* and *Coffin Texts* that occur first in the same sequence on early second-millennium coffins. The late sources, on papyri, name the Osiris temple library as the connecting link in the astonishing transmission of the series across one and a half thousand years. These *sakhu*, like other groups of *Coffin Texts* that fell out of usage, form connected series of pronouncements that would have been spoken in the rites performed from death to burial; part of the rites involved an hourly watch over the dead body, in which the deceased takes the role of the murdered Osiris and the officiants become the deities that mourned him and prepared the means of his resurrection, the embalming of the body.

After *c.* 1800 BC the custom of including funerary texts in the burial was dropped, to be replaced by figures of animals (perhaps representing the forces of disorder to be overcome) and by items used to protect mother and child, such as ivory markers, as appropriate to rebirth after death as to first birth in this life. One of the later *Coffin Texts*, found on the Bersha coffin of Gua (*c.* 1850 BC), prescribes making a wooden figure of a man to do work on behalf of a person in the next world, with a text that reads:

O figure of (name of deceased), if I am summoned, if I am registered to do any work that is wont to be done in the underworld, then the task will be transposed to you there, as a person to his duty. Apply yourself in my place at any moment to cultivate the fields, irrigate the banks, transport sand from east to west. 'Here I am!' you shall say.

From *c.* 1800 BC figures of the deceased, and even in one instance a small shrine for a group of people, bore this text, which gives the name for this type of figure as *shabti* or *ushabti* at various periods. Despite the directions given in the *Coffin Texts* the figures are more often of stone or glazed composition than wood, although the Egyptians did produce crude examples of tamarisk at Thebes in the early sixteenth century BC, and brightly painted wooden *shabtis* survive from the Ramesside Period. The *shabti* remained in vogue until the Ptolemaic Period; from *c.* 1350–850 BC, and again in the seventh to sixth and in the fourth centuries BC the richer burials contained not one but dozens and even hundreds of these figures, often placed in special *shabti* boxes of wood. The most complete sets contained one for each day of the year with one 'overseer *shabti*' to keep each set of ten in order, like a workgang in daily life.

Funerary literature in tombs returns to the surviving record *c.* 1600 BC, when the royal family at Thebes had coffins with texts in part drawn from the local tradition of *Coffin Texts* but in part presenting new compositions that have no known precursors; in the absence of funerary texts for kings since *c.* 2100 BC and for others since *c.* 1800 BC, it is difficult to determine the date at which the new texts were composed. They belong firmly in the bounds of the *Coffin Texts*, with texts for the cultivation of fields, for *shabtis*, for taking any form that the deceased desires, for knowing the powers of ancient cult centres, and for identifying with the creator; yet they include substantially new features, most importantly the judgment of the dead as a way to new life. It is possible that the *Book of the Dead*, the new compilation of 'incantations for going out by day in the necropolis', does not long antedate the earliest surviving copies, on the coffins of queen Mentuhotep and prince Herunefer *c.* 1600 BC. A logical moment for compiling a new set of funerary texts would have been the division of the land *c.* 1650 BC between the old line of kings, now constrained to withdraw south to Thebes, and Semitic rulers in the north-eastern Delta, the *heqau khasut* or 'rulers of hill-lands', rendered Hyksos by the Greeks. The new corpus may also have been used for kings from the outset, and was

93 An early *shabti* figure, in this case from the substitute burial of the official escort Renseneb beneath an offering-chapel at Abydos. Some of the hieroglyphs have been modified to prevent placing potentially disruptive animals or birds directly in contact with the body or its substitute (birds with no legs, for example.) The text is highlighted in blue pigment against the white stone. Late Middle Kingdom, *c.* 1750 BC; painted limestone, from Abydos. H. 23 cm. EA 49343.

49343

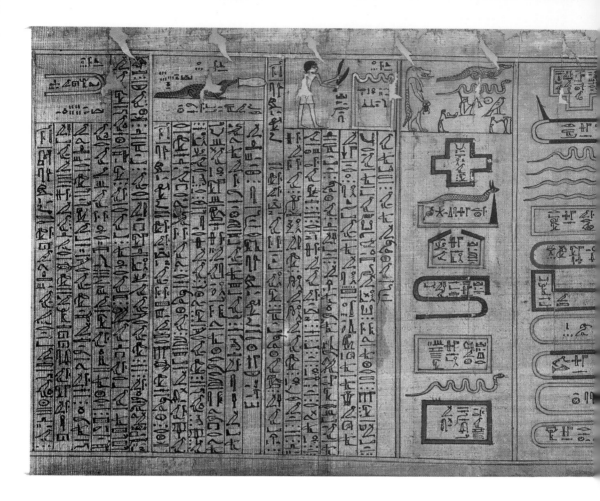

certainly included on the shroud of Thutmose III placed in his coffin by order of his son and successor Amenhotep II. Fragments of the shroud of a king Intef *c*. 1600 BC bear funerary texts but are too small to allow identification of the contents.

The new concepts of a judgment of the dead may have been formulated earlier, but it seems to me unlikely that they existed *c*. 1800 BC when the *Coffin Texts* were still in use with the old view of an afterlife without a judgment of the dead. In the *Coffin Texts* the tribunal in the afterlife was a standard court in which the divine authorities could give hearings for cases of complaint. In the new tradition the judgment of the dead was not the trial for one incident as in a modern lawcourt but an assessment of the entire being, the entire earthly life, of an individual. Each person was taken after death before Osiris, god of the dead, and his or her heart weighed on scales against the figure of the goddess Right; the good passed through to the new life as transfigured spirits, but the hearts of the wicked were tossed to Amemet, 'the swallower', portrayed with the rear of a hippopotamus, the fore of a lion and the head of a crocodile. At judgment the deceased had to declare his spiritual baggage, in a list of denials which Egyptologists call the 'negative confession'; forty-two deities heard the deceased protest innocence of crimes against the divine and the human social order, from sexual misconduct to lying and cheating to

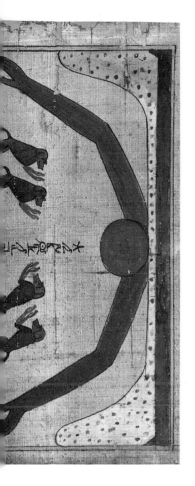

94 The end of the *Book of the Dead* of Userhat, dated stylistically to the earliest phase of writing funerary texts on papyrus for deposit in the burial. The last text in the manuscript, as most often on 18th Dynasty papyri, is the description of 'mounds' or regions of the Underworld, each with its guardian demons. The papyrus closes with a vignette of 'adoration of the sun-god at his rising', showing the arms of the horizon mountain embracing the disk as it is adored by four baboons. 18th Dynasty, $c.$ 1400 BC; painted papyrus, from Thebes. H. 33 cm. EA 10009, part.

blasphemy. Those who were found to have spoken these words truthfully were declared 'true-of-voice', on the model of Horus who was vindicated against Seth. After $c.$ 1600 BC, when the new corpus appears on coffins, the texts were written on the shrouds for Thebans both in and outside the royal family; from the reign of Hatshepsut onwards they were more often on the traditional manuscript materials of papyrus and, at first, prepared animal skins, though the latter seem not to have been used for these or other texts after $c.$ 1300 BC. The same texts can also appear on tomb-chapel and burial chamber walls, including, from the reign of Merenptah, those of the king. It is possible that earlier royal burials other than that of Thutmose III included parts of the corpus on the shroud originally placed over the body within the coffin, a source that rarely survives.

Whatever the role of that group of texts in the royal burial, the tombs of the kings are distinguished from those of their subjects by the royal *Underworld Books* reserved for the royal tomb from $c.$ 1450 to 1150 BC. As with the more widespread corpus of funerary texts, the date of composition of the *Underworld Books* is lost in the absence of the royal funerary literature of 2100–1450 BC but the texts may be separated into an earlier and later group, and it is possible that the later came into existence only shortly before it first appears in the record. Curiously the earliest source for the new royal texts is the tomb of Useramun, not king but vizier under Hatshepsut; it is possible that the queen herself planned to include different texts in her tomb, but her burial survives in too damaged a state to support or refute this. The earliest *Underworld Book* is now called the *Amduat* from the eleventh-century BC title 'book of *imy-duat*', that is, of 'what is in the Underworld', although its early title in the royal tombs was 'text of the hidden chamber'. It is the dominant feature of the tomb of the king from the reign of Thutmose III to that of Akhenaten and describes the journey of the sun-god in his boat across the twelve hours of the night to be born in the last hour through the body of a serpent to the new life of sunrise. This circuit will be joined by the king at death when he flies to the sky and merges with the sun-disk, in the words of the *Tale of Sinuhe*. In addition to parts of the *Book of the Dead* the funerary shroud of Thutmose III also bore the 'book of the adoration of Ra', now called the *Litany of Ra*, in which the different features of the divine world are adored as forms of the sun-god. Pillars in the tomb of the king complete the text on the shroud, and Sety I and later Ramesside kings had the text inscribed on the walls of their tombs.

Akhenaten excluded any divine force outside the sole disk of the sun, and his tomb at Akhetaten accordingly contained scenes only of the royal family and their own births and deaths. In the restoration against Akhenaten after his death the texts and images took on renewed vigour, seen in unparalleled motifs of solar and Osirian regeneration in the golden shrines of the first restoring king, the boy Tutankhamun; the texts include variants of passages from the *Book of the Dead* and for the first time the tale of Ra and the destruction of humanity. His general and second successor Horemheb replaced the old curving plan of the royal tomb with a straight linear series of corridors leading steeply down into the earth's depths; the *Amduat* gave way here to a composition without ancient title but today called the *Book of Gates*, because each of the twelve divisions of the night is now depicted as separated by a barrier. Although the twelve hours of the night remain, the *Book of Gates* adds a judgment-hall where Osiris looms over the dead, and a final scene in which the sun is born out of the primeval ocean in an eternal cycle. In comparison with the *Amduat* the *Book of Gates* greatly reduces the number of names for features of the underworld, marking a move away from one of the cardinal features of the *Coffin Texts*, the peopling of the underworld with myriad named creatures and obstacles to survival.

In the tomb of Ramses I, successor to Horemheb, the *Book of Gates* appears still as an alternative to the *Amduat*, but his son Sety I expanded the depth of the royal tomb and covered every wall with texts and figures, creating the space for both compositions as well as the ritual for opening the mouth of images. The ceiling over the sarcophagus in the largest chamber bears a vast depiction of the sky as Nut with the constellations as deities, recalling the depiction of the sky in the destruction of humanity and in the 'cenotaph' behind the Osiris temple built by the same king at Abydos. Merenptah, second successor to Sety I, had the corridor to the 'cenotaph' inscribed with the earliest surviving copy of another *Underworld Book*, the *Book of Caverns*, for which we have no ancient name. This appears in the tombs of Ramses IV, VI, VII and IX and divides the underworld into two halves of three ections each, with the sun-disk in place of the solar bark and with details of the tortures of the damned. These later Ramesside tombs contain a plethora of scenes that elaborate upon the journey of the sun beneath the earth in the night or in the skies of day and night; one set of scenes appears in part in the thirteenth-century BC tombs of Merenptah and Tausret and is then built into a more extended composition over much of the sarcophagus chamber of Ramses VI and has been given the modern name *Book of the Earth* because it concentrates on the chthonic aspect of solar resurrection with the gods Geb, Aker the lion and Tatenen the counterpart to Ptah.

It may be significant that only the *Amduat* and the *Litany of Ra* bear ancient titles; the other texts and scenes may rather constitute extracts from a pool of imagery both textual and pictorial that was available to the royal craftsmen and archivists responsible for planning the scheme of decoration for each tomb. Compositions could be made longer or shorter according to the available space, and may not in every case have had an existence outside their function as motifs for the

95 Fragment from a royal sarcophagus lid, perhaps that of Sety I, with the feathers of a winged figure and *shen*-ring in the claws of a vulture and text and a scene from the seventh hour in the journey of the sun-god through the night-sky as delineated in the funerary composition known today as the *Book of Gates*. 19th Dynasty, 13th century BC; painted calcite, from Thebes. H. 23 cm. EA 29948.

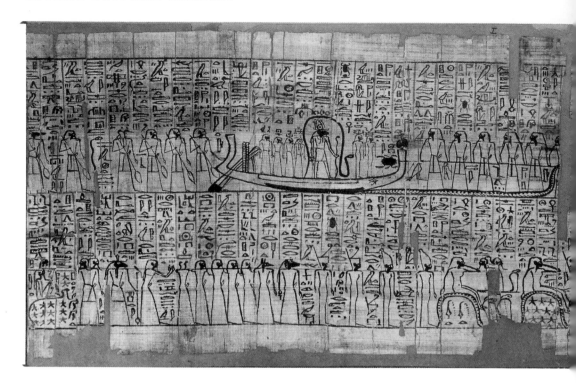

royal tomb. One of the most perfect expressions of Egyptian aestheticism, the tomb not of a king but of Nefertari, queen of Ramses II, presents a more concise summary of all that Egyptian funerary literature and indeed funerary custom sought to achieve: the rebirth identified in the sun and in the soil. The scene shows a mummiform ram-headed man supported by the goddesses Isis and her sister Nephthys, with the text 'it is Ra rested in Osiris' and 'Osiris rested in Ra'. This inspirational Ramesside image sees a solar rebirth that draws its energy from the earth and its mirror image, an earthly rebirth that draws its energy from the sun. The word-pairs material and immaterial, bodily and spiritual are inadequate to render this union that preserves the body in the earth and at the same time brings the individual to share in light. From the *ba* which is Ra in Osiris and Osiris in Ra, both king and subjects hoped to attain eternity, as sun or as transfigured spirits.

At the end of the reign of the last Ramses the rulers of Egypt agreed upon a realignment of power whereby the king resided at Tanis in the north-eastern Delta and left government of Thebes to the local authorities. The new system did not differ greatly from the previous regime except that the south no longer had gold to attract the interest of the king in the north and the king was no longer buried in Thebes. The royal tombs were now located within the precinct of the Amun temple at Tanis, and the ruling families at Thebes used existing tomb chambers for their grouped burials. Authority at Thebes was wielded by the general, sanctioned by taking the office of high priest, and the move was emulated by all other local

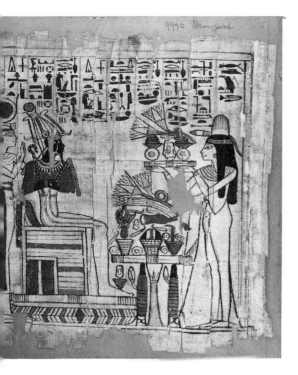

96 The text and scenes of the *Amduat*, abbreviated for the papyrus of Tentshedmut who is shown offering a table of food and flowers to Osiris and Isis. The selection here includes (left, upper register) the last episode in the *Amduat* where the sun-god, a ram-headed figure on the solar bark, achieves resurrection by being dragged through a serpent named 'Life of the gods'. 21st Dynasty, *c.* 950 BC; painted papyrus, from Thebes. H. 24.5 cm. EA 9970.

worthies. The impression of a state within a state or of a government by priests should not obscure how similar the administration remained to Ramesside and Tuthmosside government in the area. The officials of the Amun domain are now entitled priests, but do not otherwise seem to differ from their earlier counterparts and their wives continue to hold the same title of 'chantress of Amun', doubtless a valued source of income with its implicit share in temple revenue. The new system of burial marked a more substantive change; from the eleventh century BC noble burials at Thebes included not only a papyrus with 'incantations for going out by day' (*Book of the Dead*) but a second manuscript entitled *Book of what is in the Underworld*. As a rule the eleventh- and early tenth-century manuscripts contain a short version of the *Litany of Ra*, while tenth- and early ninth-century papyri give the last part of the *Amduat*, the ninth to twelfth hours as they occupy one wall of the sarcophagus chamber of Amenhotep II; that tomb was reused as a safe hiding-place or cache for some of the royal mummies at this period, and this may have provided the opportunity for copying the text once reserved for royal use. A third class of manuscripts was developed, also exclusively at Thebes, in which elements of different earlier compositions were mixed with new illustrations to form so-called vignette papyri with little text to accompany the figures. The richness of theological speculation in these papyri found equal outlet on the coffins of the same period at Thebes, the only other major item in the equipping of each burial.

In the ninth century BC the detailed decoration of Theban coffins gave way to a plainer style without texts and the local practice of placing funerary manuscripts in

167

the burial vanished altogether. At Tanis in the north meanwhile we find for the first time since Ramses XI royal burial chambers inscribed with scenes and texts extracted from the *Book of the Dead* and the *Underworld Books*. The occurrence of both startling reversals in the surviving record at the two governing centres of Egypt suggests that there may be a link to wider historical developments; the reign of Osorkon II brought a reimposition of northern control over Thebes, which resisted with force according to the Karnak inscription of the general Osorkon, a prince in the royal house. Yet the link may not amount to a direct royal clampdown on Theban use of texts because the Thebans did not resume their earlier coffin and manuscript traditions under the weak successors of Osorkon II. It is also significant that the disappearance of funerary texts involved not only those reserved before 1100 BC for the king but also the *Book of the Dead* which had always been available to his subjects. Therefore the renewed vigour of the north under Osorkon II may have caused the change in Theban burial customs more indirectly, by promoting the spread of northern textless funerary traditions to the southern city, much as funerary customs altered abruptly in the nineteenth century BC without any obvious political motivation.

Whatever the reasons for the change, for over a century no funerary literature survives, unless manuscripts lie hidden still in the wrappings of eighth-century mummies. At the end of the eighth century the kingdom of Napata, in what is today the Sudan, conquered Egypt and stimulated a revival of pre-Ramesside traditions, notably under Shabako – who had the creation text of Memphis copied from a rotting manuscript onto a slab of basalt called today the Shabako Stone – and in the early seventh century under Taharqo, who revived such compositions as the *King as Priest of the Sun*. Administrators of the estate of the 'god's wife of Amun' and the mayors of Thebes constructed over their tombs chapels on the scale of royal cult complexes. These continued to be erected under the Saite kings who ruled Egypt after the Assyrian invasions of 671, 667 and 664 BC and provided ample space for new and often faithful editions of the *Book of the Dead*, *Litany of Ra* and *Underworld Books*. In the mid-seventh century coffins also began again to bear extracts from the *Book of the Dead* and a single papyrus for a man called Nespasef survives from the same period; the manuscript of Nespasef is of particular importance because it reveals a new edition of the *Book of the Dead* quite distinct from earlier examples. Whereas the papyri of *c.* 1450–850 BC presented highly variable sequences of selected incantations from the corpus, the seventh-century version set a model sequence to which papyri of the next six centuries adhere to a remarkable extent. Curiously few manuscripts survive from the seventh and sixth centuries and none from the period of Persian occupation, but the fourth and third centuries brought a large-scale revival of funerary papyri; fourth-century Memphite burials even had the text written on the linen mummy-wrappings themselves.

In 1842 the German scholar Richard Lepsius allotted numbers to texts and some illustrations as 'chapters' in this edition of the *Book of the Dead*, a numbering system still used by Egyptologists today, and Paul Barguet has offered a coherent explanation for the particular order in which the various texts occur. According to his scheme 'chapters 1 to 16' accompany the funeral procession from embalming

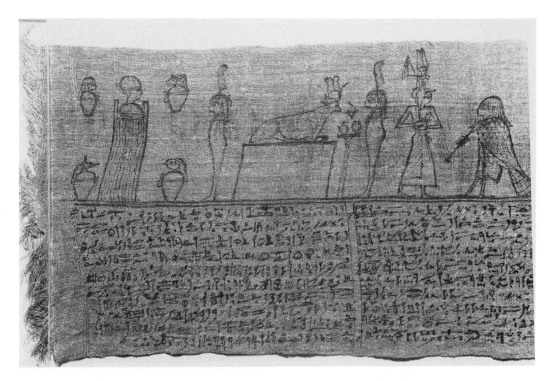

97 Texts from the *Book of the Dead* written on a mummy-wrapping of a man named Padimin. The scenes form part of the extended vignette to chapter 17 of the *Book of the Dead*, with a bearer of the figure of Min to the right, the cow representing Mehytweret 'the great flood' at the centre, and on the left a chest with the four canopic jars with heads representing the guardian deities of the entrails, Hapy (baboon), Imsety (man), Qebehsenuef (falcon) and Duamutef (jackal). 30th Dynasty, 4th century BC; linen, from Saqqara (?). H. 17 cm. EA 10826, part.

house to burial-chamber, the scene depicted in the continuous vignette running above these texts. 'Chapter 15' is a hymn to the sun, selected from various choices and '16' is the accompanying illustration, covering the full height of the papyrus roll and so marking a formal break. The next group, 'chapters 17 to 63', provide for the regeneration of the deceased by conferring on him the use of his faculties, above all his heart and mouth, as well as the power to repel harmful forces and avert decay, and the power over the elements of air, to be able to breathe, and fire, to avoid being consumed by fire, the fate of many a burial. In this group 'chapter 17' is the great creation text with commentaries, cited in chapter one of this book and 'chapters 18 to 20' seek to justify the deceased on the model of the triumph of Osiris, while 'chapter 30' often occurs separately on scarabs placed on the heart to secure its loyalty in the judgment of the dead. The third section of the edition, 'chapters 64 to 129', opens with a text which could take the place of 'chapter 30' on scarabs or be aligned with it in manuscripts; this 'chapter 64' is, like '17', a complex cosmic text in which the deceased is identified with Ra who emerges out of Osiris, the secret of resurrection. With his new powers of life the deceased receives in this section final transfiguration, including the ability to assume different shapes ('chapters 76 to 88'), to 'know the powers' of west, east, north (Buto) and south (Nekhen) and of Iunu and Khemenu and to farm the fields of the underworld ('chapters 107 to 116'). At this point the deceased gains entry into the community of the dead by passing the judgment with the weighing of the heart and the negative confession or denial of sins ('chapter 125'). The final section places the deceased as a transfigured spirit in the retinue of Ra on the solar bark ('chapters 130 to 136') and gives the geography of the underworld with its seven portals, twenty-one gateways and fourteen mounds where the gods and dead rest ('chapters 144 to 146, 149 to 150'). Other chapters here secure eternal sustenance through the heavenly bull, seven cows and four steering-oars ('chapter 148') and ensure the eternal survival of the mummified body in a properly constructed burial chamber ('chapters 151 and 152') and with its armoury of amulets ('chapters 155 to 160'). The edition closes with texts for power over the four winds ('chapter 161'), for life-giving fire under the head of the deceased, given concrete form in the fourth century BC as an inscribed circle of material, the hypocephalus ('chapter 162') and for the protection of the deceased by Theban deities (the only time that they play a role in the *Book of the Dead* and among the few texts added to the corpus after *c.* 900 BC, 'chapters 163 to 165').

Towards the end of the Ptolemaic Period full-length *Books of the Dead* were no longer produced but the shorter selections from the corpus continued to be included in burial equipment into the Roman Period. At the same time new compilations of funerary texts appeared, and these eventually replaced the *Book of the Dead*. The final flourish of the funerary text in Egypt dates to about the time that the New Testament began to be written down in the lands bordering Egypt, the late first and early second centuries AD. The most common of the late Ptolemaic and Roman Period funerary texts are entitled 'documents for breathing', and open with wording reminiscent of formal bureaucratic records, as edicts by the gods to permit the deceased new life, a literal application of the funerary papyrus as passport. The abbreviated versions could even be folded into small packets in the manner of a letter and placed at head and legs of the deceased, as in the latest surviving burial group, that of the official Soter and his family from the reign of Hadrian. The 'documents for breathing' appear to be Theban products and the second version composed in the late first century AD may even be located more specifically at the temple of Khons in Karnak since it figures particularly often in burials of priests of Khons. Here end the traditions of funerary literature that first took written form over two and a half thousand years earlier in the pyramid of Unas at Saqqara. In the second century AD the temple library at Tebtunis in the Fayum produced an astonishing revival of Pharaonic traditions in script, both hieroglyphic and cursive, but the thousands of surviving fragments do not include texts for the tomb. Within a century Egypt had converted to new burial customs, eschewing the ancient arts of mummification and all its supports in texts, images and offerings; the change at the grave reveals with mute clarity that the country had embraced a different faith and that Christ had replaced Osiris and Ra.

98 Mummy-board for the deceased woman Tentbastet with funerary scenes and text in demotic. These boards mark the end of the tradition in written Egyptian funerary literature that began in the 25th century BC with the *Pyramid Texts*. Roman Period, 1st to 2nd century AD; painted wood, of unknown provenance. H. 1.45 m. EA 35464.

EPILOGUE

Egyptian Deities Abroad

OUTSIDE EGYPT HER GODS AND GODDESSES enjoyed a varied reception through the ages. For themselves the Egyptians set up shrines for their deities on foreign soil on the exceptional occasions when they left their homeland; expeditions to quarry or mine materials on a regular basis set up shrines at their destination, for example to Hathor mistress of turquoise at Serabit el-Khadim in Sinai, and to Min as deity of the eastern deserts at the galena mines on the Red Sea coast at Gebel Zeit. More permanent foreign settlements occupied by the Egyptians might also become home to Egyptian deities, as in Gaza where Ramses III built a sanctuary for Amun. The cult of Hathor at Byblos apparently arose out of trading contacts whereby the Levantine port served as the general point of entry for Egypt into the rich markets of the Near East. The most complete absorption of Egyptian cults took place in the land held by the Pharaohs for the longest time, Nubia to the south; there the conquering Middle Kingdom Pharaohs Senusret I and III installed a temple of Horus at Buhen and themselves received worship in the New Kingdom, when Amenhotep III and Ramses II also implanted the cult of themselves alongside that of Amun, Ra, Ptah and Hathor. In the other direction the Egyptians proved less receptive to Nubian gods, only Dedwen the bringer of incense appearing on monuments from the Delta to Elephantine. By contrast Egyptian monuments and names of the New Kingdom often cite Western Asiatic deities such as Baal, Reshep, Hurun and Qedeshet, reflecting the settlement of foreigners in Egypt.

In the eighth century BC the kingdom centred on Napata in the Sudan adopted Egyptian cults, script and principles of art to express its power, rising to engulf

99 Stela in the Egyptian style with Greek influence, particularly noticeable in the costume of the deceased on the lower register. The script of the text reveals that this was set up for a member of the Memphite community from the Western Anatolian land of Caria. In the central register appears the Apis bull of Ptah between Hathor or Isis and Thoth; above the deceased worships Osiris who is protected by Isis under the winged sun-disk with uraei. Late Period, after 600 BC; limestone, from Saqqara. H. 62 cm. EA 67235.

Egypt itself by the end of that century. The Theban god Amun was worshipped at Gebel Barkal at a New Kingdom site, and the 'sacred mountain' there became a focus for state patronage of the Amun cult. Alongside Egyptian deities the Napatan kings and, from the sixth century BC, their successors based at Meroe revered Nubian deities sometimes with Nubian names such as the lion deity Apedemak, sometimes with an Egyptian form such as Iryhemesnefer 'good companion' (rendered in a Greek text as Arensnuphis). From the fourth century BC Egyptian sanctuaries were built south of Elephantine at sites from Philae to Kalabsha and here some Meroitic deities received worship in Ptolemaic and Roman times, but they seem not to have penetrated farther north. The temple of Isis at Philae remained in operation later than most sanctuaries in Egypt partly because the nomads of the south-eastern desert retained their devotion to the goddess; a sacred falcon resided on the island until the Byzantine emperor Justinian ordered the closure of the temple in the sixth century AD. In the kingdoms to the south Christianity took longer to gain dominance over earlier beliefs, but the realm of Meroe had by this stage vanished and with it the initiative for major architectural ventures such as temples.

The first millennium BC witnessed the spread of Egyptian deities to the north as well. Here again, as in Nubia, they found new settings, and thus new roles and characters. Just as Amun is not in Nubia precisely the same deity he could be in Egypt, given the difference in his entourage in the two places, so deities such as Isis and Osiris had a subtly transposed character when they became part of a different world, that of Greece and then Rome. The diffusion of Egyptian deities began in the first half of the first millennium BC, as attested by bronze and faience figures found on archaeological sites throughout the Mediterranean from Spain to the Aegean. The latter became strategically vital to Egypt in the seventh to fourth centuries BC, when succeeding Pharaohs put their hopes of military strength in Greek alliances and mercenary forces. The account by Herodotus of particularly close links between Samos and Egypt in the reign of Ahmose II is borne out by the discovery of Egyptian bronzes in the temple of Hera on Samos; some bronzes date to the period before the seventh and sixth centuries, although it is uncertain when they left Egypt. In the evidence for Egyptian deities in the Mediterranean arena this earlier history of archaeological finds indicates contact, direct or indirect, with Egypt and even the acceptance abroad of Egyptian iconography, exported on the trade-routes of the Greeks and the Phoenicians; Phoenician art itself incorporated many of the motifs from monuments of Egyptian cult and kingship.

The early phase anticipated a second still more striking development, the creation of shrines devoted specifically to Egyptian deities rather than just harbouring Egyptian images in the context of a local cult; the fourth century BC appears to have prepared the ground for this development, as indicated by reference to a temple of Isis founded by Egyptians by 333 BC at Pirrhaeus, the port of Athens, precisely the type of trading milieu to foster the growth of such imported religious practice. When the Macedonian king Alexander the Great defeated the Persian Empire in 332 BC he incorporated into his new Greek-speaking realm all its provinces, including Egypt which had been conquered by the Persians for the second time only a decade before. As part of the Macedonian Empire of Alexander and then under the separate rule of the Macedonian general Ptolemy and his successors, Egypt found itself oriented northward as never before. The kingdom of Ptolemy kept its capital at Alexandria on the north-west seashore of the Delta and directly governed not only Cyprus, long exposed to trade with and influence of Egypt, but also parts of the Aegean, affording Egyptian cults new status in the Greek world as part of state-sponsored religion.

Within Egypt the Ptolemies built in part in Greek style, as in the immense classical Greek temple at Khemenu in Middle Egypt, and in part on traditional Egyptian models as they stood under the fourth-century Pharaohs. The projects of the last of those, Nakhthorheb, were continued and expanded. The scale of royal expenditure was scarcely equalled in earlier times, as seen above all in the magnificent sanctuaries created under the Ptolemies at Philae, Edfu and Dendera, all of which concentrated divine and royal cult at the same focus; the combination of the two received architectural expression in the 'birth-houses', a shrine adjacent to the main temple in which, since Nakhtnebef, the divine birth of the king became enshrined in the cult as the birth of the child of the principal god and goddess to form the classic late pattern of a temple triad. Another move to cement royal cult throughout Egypt also became prominent under the fourth-century Pharaohs, particularly Nakhthorheb, namely the practice of mummifying certain species of animal and bird for burial in catacombs. The practice flourished in the Ptolemaic and Roman Periods, by which time the burial place of the ibis at Saqqara, to take a typical example, housed a staggering horde of birds, estimated by the excavators at no less than four million. The royal decrees promulgated concerning the animal and bird burials and cults serve as a reminder that in Egypt all cult was in a sense royal cult, since Pharaoh alone was in direct communion with the gods as the one who offered to them and received blessings from them on a cosmic, eternal level. The king ousted by the second Persian conquest in 343 BC, Nakhthorheb, himself received worship as Nakhthorheb-the-falcon, a vivid recasting of the theme that the king is Horus and that Horus is the *ka* of the king.

The Egyptian sanctuaries in the Greek-speaking world built equally strongly on fourth-century precedent; by 200 BC Egyptian shrines existed at such sites as Eretria, Salamis, Delos and Priene, and the next two centuries saw the cults spread to Sicily, southern Italy and Iberia, with a temple of Isis installed at Pompeii in the mid-second century BC. Rome itself and its port at Ostia became home to numerous shrines to Egyptian deities during the first century BC, including one of the largest temples to Isis, that on the Field of Mars; this Iseum Campense underwent a dramatic series of transformations in the first century AD, being closed after a scandal in the reign of Tiberius, reopened under Caligula and reconstructed on a suitably imperial scale in the reign of Domitian in AD 80. The complex of temples occupied a site at the modern festival square of Rome, the Piazza Navona, with an avenue of sculpture connecting the temples of Isis and Serapis marked by sphinxes, lions and obelisks brought from Egypt and, in some cases, actually commissioned for the building rather than merely being reused earlier monuments. Domitian also constructed a new temple to Isis in Benevento, at the crossroads of inland trade-

100 and 101 Ibis mummies (OPPOSITE) and a stela (LEFT) representing a mummified falcon in a shrine with winged sun-disks; on either side appears a cobra on heraldic plant, one for Upper and one for Lower Egypt. The study of these testimonies to Late Period animal and bird catacombs has been hampered until recent years by the lack of systematic excavation and recording. Ptolemaic Period, 3rd century BC or later. Shrine-stela of painted limestone, unknown provenance. H. 37.5 cm. EA 49734. Mummies, from Abydos. H. of right mummy 26 cm. EA 52927, 53937.

routes across southern Italy, similarly fitted with an avenue of sphinxes, obelisks and sculpture of the Apis bull, falcons and baboons. The Roman Empire embraced Egyptian cults at all levels, from the imperial temples in the capital to shrines at military garrisons as distant as York and London to household shrines such as the fabulous painted room in the Pompeii villa now known as the 'House of the Mysteries'. This devotion was strongly demonstrated for the last time in the third century AD under Septimius Severus and his successors, who were also among the last emperors to support hieroglyphic workshops and so the productive kernel of Pharaonic religion within Egypt itself. During the fourth century, outside as well as inside their land of origin, the Egyptian cults were eclipsed by new devotion to Mithras, the invincible sun and, increasingly, by a new Jewish sect, Christianity.

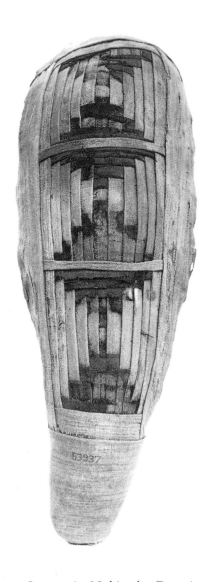
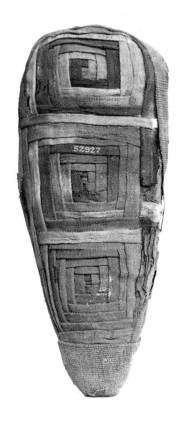

Just as in Nubia the Egyptian deities outside Egypt did not form the same pantheon as at home under the Pharaohs, only a small number of deities found favour abroad and they were inserted there into local patterns of belief and non-Egyptian aspirations and practices. The main deities worshipped in the ancient Greek and Latin world, particularly in the heyday of these cults from the third century BC to the third century AD, were those in human form – Isis and a new interpretation of Osiris called Serapis. Serapis was the Greek rendering of Egyptian 'Osir-Apis', that is, the Osiris (i.e. deceased) Apis, a term used in the reign of Nakhthorheb to refer to the Apis bull at Memphis through which Ptah and the creative forces of the earth could be served in this world. Under the Ptolemies Serapis became a principal god of Alexandria as deity of the fertile earth, and received a new form in Greek depiction as a bearded man wearing on his head a grain-measure to symbolise his fruitfulness. The theme drew on the perception of Osiris as grain-god, seen in the sarcophagus texts of Ankhnesneferibra, as much as from the Pharaonic cult of the Apis bull. In Alexandria and throughout the Greek- and then the Latin-speaking world, Isis and Serapis came to embody a pair of natural forces of fertility, male and female. The protecting serpents of the home could in Alexandrian iconography take the form of a pair of human-headed serpents, one for each door-jamb, one bearded male as Serapis and one female for Isis.

The rites for innumerable shrines were modelled in part on Egyptian precedent, not surprisingly since the cults were first installed by men of Egyptian birth, such as the Memphite priest who introduced the cult of Serapis to Delos in the early third century BC, according to an inscription set up by his nephew at the dedication of a new Serapeum there. Water for the purification rituals at the Iseum Campense was imported from the Nile, in a move to emphasise the presence of Osiris in the river after his death, and the human-headed vase later confused with the vases containing embalmed internal organs of the body was borne in processions. Festivals marked the death of Osiris and his mourning by Isis, with autumn harvest feasts on an Egyptian pattern with the full story as related by Plutarch re-enacted from the murder of the god to his resurrection by Isis; these episodes probably constituted the Isia celebrated in Rome from 28 October to 1 November, followed by the Hilaria or festival of joy on 3 November, for the rediscovery of the god. The festival of the resurrection of Osiris was still being celebrated at Faleria in Etruria in AD 417. Other festivals had Greek origins, such as the sailing of Isis celebrated in the Roman Period at ports such as Naples and Byzantium, where Isis as patron of seafaring seems to have presided over an earlier Greek ceremony.

The principal difference between Egyptian and foreign cults of Egyptian deities lay in their application to society. In Egypt the priests had, according to Ptolemaic texts on temple walls, to be pure and refrain from the same transgressions as those listed in the 'negative confession' at the judgment of the dead; the purified could then perform the rites necessary to the cult, that is touching the sacred image as it is clothed and fed in the daily ritual and as it is transferred from the temple on festival processions. The cult serviced the universe in a mechanical manner, enabling the king, locally through priests, to keep alive the community of humanity with the world it inhabits. In Greek and Roman tradition Egyptian deities, and above all Isis, played a role more universal and at the same time more personal; the goddess was available to all who would be her followers and those who served her gained personal redemption. In the second century AD Apuleius wrote an autobiographical account of the Isis cult from the vantagepoint of an initiate, in which the Egyptian detail may be contrasted with the Graeco-Roman emphasis on the human

102 Stela of the Roman Emperor Tiberius offering a figure of Right (Maat) to the Theban triad (Amun, Mut and Khons) upon the restoration of the Mut enclosure-wall, as celebrated in the hieroglyphic text. Roman Period, c. AD 25; sandstone, from Thebes. H. 66 cm. EA 1432.

rather than cosmic. The initiate had to acknowledge the sinfulness of certain actions, in particular 'enslaving desires' to be replaced by the desire for Isis and 'adverse curiosity' to be countered by the 'quest for truth'; only those deemed capable of the proper behaviour could enter the community of initiates, and the successful applicant was then shown sacred Egyptian texts kept in the sanctuary and underwent a night-time ritual, passing through the underworld and the elements to see the radiant sun in the middle of the night. From the night of initiation the person emerged like the sun at dawn, a close parallel to the New Kingdom royal *Underworld Books* where too the passage of the sun through the night brings in the union of light and darkness, Ra and Osiris, a new life. By opening the mysteries of the underworld from a circle of temple technicians to all who wished to become initiates, the Greek and Roman arena converted Egyptian practice into a different means of approaching gods, one close enough to merge entirely with the rival mystery religions in the Roman Empire during the fourth century AD.

Christianity swamped Egyptian religion both in its native and in its Hellenistic and Roman forms by the fifth century, with few references to the old gods and goddesses after the division of the Empire into a western Roman and an eastern Byzantine half. The lifeblood of practices expressing beliefs is as much the space, that is the architecture, in which they take place as the intent of the individual believers practising the faith. When the Roman emperors ceased to underwrite first, in the third century AD, Egyptian style temples and then, in the fourth century AD, any temples, they removed the institutions of service by which the practices were kept alive from generation to generation. A surviving practice requires an institution of some order if it is not to change and in Egypt the means of making a practice permanent, of changing it into an institution, were text and image. With the evaporation of workshops for the production of texts and images according to the proper forms, the expression of beliefs automatically had to change. In this air of innovation Egypt had already to a large extent embraced a new means of expressing funerary and ritual concerns, in a style less harmonious but no less powerful than Pharaonic art; perhaps this prepared the ground for a new alien tradition in Egypt itself in the dramatic conversion of the country between AD 250 and 450.

The conversion of Egypt and the Roman Empire severed any concrete links to the traditions of Pharaonic civilisation in the perception, naming and depiction of separate aspects of divinity; all gods were now one, not the visible sun-disk of Akhenaten but the hidden universal power to which, in the Egyptian pantheon, Amun comes the nearest. The Pharaonic monuments, like those of the Greeks and Romans, became targets of a defacing programme similar to those conducted two thousand years earlier against Hatshepsut, Amun and finally Akhenaten. Whereas the Pharaonic erasure programme aimed at names and complete images, the Christian agents often defaced only head, wrists and ankles, because the hieroglyphs could no longer be read and because they deemed it sufficient to disable the figures that now represented powers of darkness. Against the official condemnation of polytheism a subversive folklore grew up for the first time, in the form of local practices to secure the protection of ancient deities or their cult centres. Even modern times have witnessed such survivals as the practice of touching ancient statues or praying and dancing at temples by women hoping for successful pregnancy. These activities, like the Greek and Roman cults of Egyptian deities, belong to a new social setting with different choices available to members of the community and a different social profile for each of those choices; their connection with the Pharaonic past is at best indirect.

In AD 394 the latest known ancient text in hieroglyphs was inscribed at Philae; thereafter a few festivals are mentioned at temples such as Memphis, but the Christian Church had long since interpreted the world for society by the time that Justinian had Philae closed to worship of gods and goddesses. A few ancient emblems were incorporated into Egyptian Christianity and the Egyptian language was now written in Greek letters with a supplement of cursive signs derived from hieroglyphs, but the rule prevailed forbidding Pharaonic principles of depiction on either large or small scale, as 'art' or 'writing'. Paradoxically the Egyptian cross, most frequent of all Christian motifs, often takes the shape of an old sign of life, implanting the old world at the heart of the new. Egypt fostered the first monasteries and Egyptian monks brought their brand of fervour across to some surprising corners of the Western Roman Empire; the Swiss town of St Maurice takes its name from an Egyptian named Mauritius, said to have been martyred with a garrison of Thebes in AD 285, and the three headless saints on the coat-of-arms of Zurich are three more Egyptians, Felix, Regula and Exuperantius. Some sources take the connection still farther, beyond the borders of the Roman Empire to the shores of Scotland and Ireland, in the tradition that both civilisation and the stone of Scone were brought by Gathelus and Scota the daughter of Pharaoh. More tangible links may be found in the Book of Leinster where 'the seven Egyptian monks in Disert Ullaigh' are invoked, and in the geography written by the Irish monk Dicuil who claimed to have learned of Egypt from a fellow monk. Whatever the substance in these elusive ties, Ireland became the second home of monasticism on the model established in the Egyptian deserts.

Despite Christianisation and the physical distance from the Nile Valley, compounded after AD 641 by the Islamic conquest of Egypt and its subsequent conversion to a new faith, Western Europe retained some impression of the Pharaohs if only through the mostly hostile testimony of the Bible in the stories of Joseph and Moses. Direct contact became rare in the turbulent waters of the Mediterranean where piracy, suppressed by the Romans, returned as Saracen ships preyed on shipping, especially from Christian Europe. Nevertheless some merchants continued to brave the journey to Islamic Alexandria, where the Ayyubite Sultans granted two depots to Venetian traders, alone of all Europeans, in the early thirteenth century, precisely when the Christian holy wars – the crusades – had put the Middle East back on the European map though in conditions of extreme antagonism. Paradoxically the next great Islamic conquest, the capture of Constantinople/Byzantium in 1453, gave Western Europe a new source of information on the very world that it made less accessible; in the wake of Ottoman Turkish occupation, Byzantine scholars and their precious manuscripts fled to the Latin West, encouraging a new interest in classical Greek sources. In the emerging cities of the Renaissance the new movement found a ready audience; already in 1419 the text *Hieroglyphica* had been found, an ancient version in Greek of the treatise on hieroglyphs by an Egyptian priest Horapollon, that is, Hor in Egyptian and in Greek the deity equated with Horus, Apollo. In the scholarly revival of Greek literature during the late fifteenth century the discovery of manuscripts coincided with far swifter methods of communicating texts to a wide audience, the invention of printing; written works on Egypt included those of Diodorus, published in Latin in 1472, and Herodotus, published in Greek in 1474.

The literary rediscovery assisted an artistic revival in which, to take the most celebrated example, Pintoricchio painted a series of frescos on the theme of the Apis bull adorning the coat-of-arms of Pope Alexander VI; the motif alluded to a legend recounted by Diodorus in which Osiris became king of Italy. Papal Rome also brought the Pharaonic past back into prominence through the extraordinary feats of engineering in the raising of the obelisks brought to the city by the Roman emperors. Domenico Fontana undertook the re-erection in 1586 of the obelisk from the Circus Vaticanus to provide a focus before the new Basilica of St Peter by Michelangelo and followed this triumph with the reconstruction and erection in 1588 of an obelisk in front of the cathedral of Rome, the Lateran basilica of St John, and the raising of a third obelisk at the centre of the Piazza del Popolo in 1589. These public demonstrations of the power of Egyptian monuments stimulated interest throughout the learned European world, but even the brilliance of Fontana seems overshadowed by Bernini who created a Baroque fountain in 1648 to 1651 out of another obelisk, this time raised from the Iseum Campense, to adorn the Piazza Navona for Pope Innocent X whose residence looked onto the square. Italy and particularly Rome abounded in Egyptian antiquities commissioned or brought out of Egypt by the Julio-Claudian and Flavian emperors. Some objects were, however, not Egyptian but inspired by Egypt, above all those for the Isis cult such as the inlaid bronze panel which was known as the Mensa Isiaca and was in the collection of Cardinal Pietro Bembo in the early sixteenth century. The Egyptianising antiquities could not at that stage be distinguished from actual Egyptian products, a reminder of how varied and complex the links of Egypt to Europe can prove. The discussion of the figures on the Mensa Isiaca distracted scholars searching for the meaning of Pharaonic art and hieroglyphs for the next three centuries. The seventeenth-century Jesuit scholar Athanasius Kircher dedicated much of his time and considerable talent to the quest to understand ancient Egypt in her monuments and scripts, formed a Museum Kircherianum and made the important connection between ancient Egyptian and Coptic, that is, the language and script of Christians in Egypt. Yet the limited amount of published material did not permit any advance beyond speculation and Kircher is often remembered by modern scholars for his elaborate symbolic interpretations of even the smallest and simplest groups of signs.

Italy did not yield the only Egyptian antiquities or the only travellers to brave the seas to Alexandria and the Nile. In 1632 two Ptolemaic sarcophagi were imported to Marseilles and entered the collection of Nicolas Fouquet, while another Provencal antiquarian, Nicolas-Claude Fabri de Peiresc (1580–1637), gathered at Aix the most substantial gallery of antiquities and himself inspired Father Kircher to study ancient Egypt. In 1646 the English astronomer John Greaves published an account of his visit seven years earlier to the pyramids of Giza, complete with his measurements and references to earlier authors including, unlike more recent scientific books, works by Arabic scholars. In these travels and publications the Pharaonic past of Egypt was coming back to life, yet still through alien eyes; the Renaissance and Baroque approached ancient Egypt as an exotic land of symbols through the often obfuscating remarks of Biblical and classical Greek and Roman texts. Travellers brought their stories and the monuments back not into a neutral vacuum but to a learned and curious public with abundant preconceptions and expectations. The European enlightenment in the eighteenth century provided the same ambivalent environment to absorb rediscoveries such as the identification of Thebes by Father Claude Sicard in 1718. In 1731 the abbé Jean Terrasson published his didactic novel *Séthos* on the path to enlightenment taken by an Egyptian priest and the book became a bestseller of its time, spawning both the literary offshoots such as *Thamos, king of Egypt* by Tobias Gebler (1773) and its musical successor, the *Magic Flute* of Emmanuel Schikaneder and Wolfgang Amadeus Mozart (1793). The Terrasson novel may also have encouraged within the burgeoning masonic movement the development of rituals for the worship of divine wisdom through Isis and Osiris; the classical antecedents seem clear in the writings of Plutarch and Apuleius, and the final product is as simultaneously Egyptian and un-Egyptian as the Isis mysteries of ancient Greek and Roman times.

Misunderstanding of the Pharaonic past could only be dispelled by the monuments and texts themselves and these began to be imported into Europe out of Ottoman Egypt in increasing numbers during the eighteenth century as kings and noblemen joined in the enthusiasm for this part of the past. Major expeditions to the Nile were undertaken by the Dane Frederik Norden in 1737-8, and the Englishman Richard Pococke and the Scot James Bruce in 1771-2, the latter penetrating deep into the Sudan and even to Ethiopia. Yet nothing prepared either Egypt or Europe for the scale of renewed ties that followed the expedition of Bonaparte as first consul of the new French Republic in 1798 to 1801; the expedition met military failure at the hands of local resistance and British and Ottoman counterattack but it destabilised the feudal power of the Mameluke overlords of Egypt and brought back to Europe a wealth of monuments and, equally vital, accurate drawings. Monuments included the Rosetta Stone, a basalt stela fragment with the same text in Egyptian and Greek, firing a new generation of scholars with the zeal to decipher the hieroglyphs. The publication of the drawings and scientific notes involved a vast printing operation that extended from 1809 through the fall, rise and fall of Napoleon and his empire, to the end of restored Bourbon rule in France in 1830. The wave of fresh material in print and in the original surged forth in the peace that followed Waterloo in 1815, when travel to and in Egypt became easier than at any time since the break-up of the Roman Empire. Within Egypt itself relative stability was assured by the iron rule of the Ottoman governor, an Albanian named Mohammed Ali, who fostered European contacts in the interests of modernisation. The representatives of the European powers, Middle Eastern

103 Block-statue of the high priest Ry, one of the finest pieces found by the French expedition and brought back to Europe. At the time it was discovered, the hieroglyphs could not be read and the art was so imperfectly understood that the soft features of the face deceived the early 19th-century scholars into thinking that it represented a woman. 19th Dynasty, *c*. 1250 BC; grey granite, from the Mut Temple at Karnak, Thebes. H. 88 cm. EA 81.

adventurers entitled consuls at the court of Mohammed Ali, invested time and resources in amassing antiquities to offer to their own or other governments; thus were formed the nuclei of national museums in London, Paris, Turin, Berlin and Leiden, as of a host of less extensive collections. With such quantity and quality of Egyptian products before their eyes, the scholarly and wider public could scarcely dismiss any longer the ancient East as the estranged lands divorced from Europe by Biblical and Latin disapproval.

In 1818 the great statue of Ramses II known as the Younger Memnon was installed in the British Museum by gift of the consul Henry Salt and the Swiss explorer Johann Burkhardt; in 1822 the young French scholar Jean-François Champollion deciphered the hieroglyphs by recognising, for the first time in one and a half thousand years, that they combined signs to represent sound with signs to represent ideas. The two events are not connected directly but stand emblematic of the sea-change in European contact with Pharaonic Egypt. In 1824 Champollion published his *Précis* of the grammar of hieroglyphic texts, enabling modern scholars to read ancient Egypt more on its own terms and less through the prejudicial and distorting perspective of Europe. The task of understanding and remembering had been launched, and it continues in the search for the past, for the context of texts, objects and images. The names and shapes of the gods and goddesses can now, if we wish, emerge from the shadow of difference to reveal the hopes and fears of the ancient Egyptians.

Chronology

(Overlapping dates usually indicate coregencies. All dates before 664 BC are approximate.)

First Dynasty	*c.* 3100–2890 BC
Second Dynasty	*c.* 2890–2686 BC
Third Dynasty	*c.* 2686–2613 BC
Fourth Dynasty	*c.* 2613–2494 BC
Fifth Dynasty	*c.* 2494–2345 BC
Sixth Dynasty	*c.* 2345–2181 BC
Seventh/Eighth Dynasties	*c.* 2181–2125 BC
Ninth/Tenth Dynasties	*c.* 2160–2130 BC, *c.* 2125–2025 BC
Eleventh Dynasty	*c.* 2125–1985 BC
Twelfth Dynasty	*c.* 1985–1795 BC
Thirteenth Dynasty	*c.* 1795–*c.* 1650 BC
Fourteenth Dynasty	*c.* 1750–*c.* 1650 BC
Fifteenth Dynasty (Hyksos)	*c.* 1650–1550 BC
Sixteenth Dynasty	*c.* 1650–*c.* 1550 BC
Seventeenth Dynasty	*c.* 1650–1550 BC
Eighteenth Dynasty	*c.* 1550–1295 BC
Nineteenth Dynasty	*c.* 1295–1186 BC
Twentieth Dynasty	*c.* 1186–1069 BC
Twenty-first Dynasty	*c.* 1069–945 BC
Twenty-second Dynasty	*c.* 945–715 BC
Twenty-third Dynasty	*c.* 818–715 BC
Twenty-fourth Dynasty	*c.* 727–715 BC
Twenty-fifth Dynasty (Nubian or Kushite)	*c.* 747–656 BC
Twenty-sixth Dynasty (Saite)	664–525 BC
Twenty-seventh Dynasty (Persian kings)	525–404 BC
Twenty-eighth Dynasty	404–399 BC
Twenty-ninth Dynasty	399–380 BC
Thirtieth Dynasty	380–343 BC
Persian Kings	343–332 BC
Macedonian Kings	332–305 BC
The Ptolemies	305–30 BC

Bibliography

C. Aldred, *Akhenaten, King of Egypt*, London 1988

J. P. Allen, *Genesis in Egypt: The Philosophy of Ancient Egyptian Creation Accounts* (Yale Egyptological Series 2), New Haven 1988

J. P. Allen, J. Assmann *et al.*, *Religion and Philosophy in Ancient Egypt* (Yale Egyptological Series 3), New Haven 1989

C. A. R. Andrews, *Egyptian Mummies*, London 1984

I. E. S. Edwards, *The Pyramids of Egypt*, London 1978

A. Fakhry, *The Pyramids*, Chicago and London 1969

R. O. Faulkner, *The Ancient Egyptian Book of the Dead* (edition revised by Carol Andrews), London 1985

J. G. Griffith, *Plutarch: De Iside et Osiride. Translation and Commentary*, Swansea 1970

G. Hart, *A Dictionary of Egyptian Gods and Goddesses*, London and New York 1986

G. Hart, *Egyptian Myths*, London 1990

E. Hornung, *Conceptions of God in Ancient Egypt*, London 1983

E. Hornung, *The Valley of the Kings*, New York 1990

S. Morenz, *Egyptian Religion*, London 1973

E. Otto, *Egyptian Art and the Cults of Osiris and Amun*, London 1968

C. N. Reeves, *The Complete Tutankhamun*, London and New York 1990

S. Sauneron, *The Priests of Ancient Egypt*, London 1960; New York 1969

A. J. Spencer, *Death in Ancient Egypt*, London 1982

J. H. Taylor, *Egyptian Coffins*, Aylesbury 1989

Harco Willems, *Chests of Life. A Study of the Typology and Conceptual Development of Middle Kingdom Standard Class Coffins*, Leiden 1988

The English-speaking world still awaits translation of the following fundamental works by Jan Assmann:

Ägypten: Theologie und Frömmigkeit einer frühen Hochkultur, Stuttgart 1984

Der König als Sonnenpriester Gluckstadt 1970

Re und Amun. Die Krise des polytheistischen Weltbilds im Ägypten der 18.–20. Dynastie, Orbis Biblicus et Orientalis 51, 1983

Ma'at: Gerechtigkeit und Unsterblichkeit im alten Ägypten, Munich 1990.

One of the most stimulating accounts of Egyptian kingship remains that by O. D. Berlev, 'The Eleventh Dynasty in the history of Egypt' in Dwight W. Young, *Studies Presented to Hans Jakob Polotsky*, East Gloucester Massachussetts, 1981, pp. 361–377

Equally thought-provoking on this subject is the study by Lanny Bell, 'Luxor Temple and the cult of the royal *Ka*' in the *Journal for Near Eastern Studies* volume 44 (1985), pp. 251–294. The outstanding article on the *Pyramid Texts* in their original context is by Jürgen Osing, 'Zur Disposition der Pyramidentexte des Unas, in the *Mitteilungen des Deutschen archäologischen Instituts Abteilung Kairo* volume 42, 1986, pp. 131–144. A similar enterprise to return some order to the great mass of *Coffin Texts* is by Gunther Lapp, 'Die Papyrusvorlagen der Sargtexte', in *Studien zur altägyptischen Kultur* volume 16, 1988, pp. 171–202. For the Late Period sequence of chapters in the *Book of the Dead* a most convincing exposition is in Paul Barguet, *Le Livre des Morts*, Paris 1967.

Index

References in *italic* refer to the pages on which illustrations appear.